GRAMMAR
WARS II

How to Integrate Improvisation and Language Arts

D1364824

Tom Ready

MERIWETHER PUBLISHING LTD.
Colorado Springs, Colorado

Meriwether Publishing Ltd., Publisher
PO Box 7710
Colorado Springs, CO 80933-7710

Executive editor: Theodore O. Zapel
Editorial coordinator: Renée Congdon
Cover design: Jan Melvin

Library of Congress Cataloging-in-Publication Data

Ready, Tom, 1954-
    Grammar wars II : how to integrate improvisation and language arts /
by Thomas Allen Ready.
        p. cm.
    ISBN 1-56608-080-0 (pbk.)
1. English language--Grammar--Study and teaching. 2. Language arts.
3. Drama in education. 4. Educational games. I. Title: Grammar wars
2. II. Title: Grammar wars two. III. Title.
    LB1575.8 .R395 2002
    372.61--dc21

                                2002001709

Acknowledgments

I hope that I've referred enough to Keith Johnstone in this text for everyone to understand my indebtedness to him and his work in the resurgence of improv in the last fifty years. Additionally, to Linda Belt and Rebecca Stockley for their book *Acting Through Improv* and to the work of Bay Area TheatreSports in bringing improv and its various chameleon forms to my attention.

As always I have to thank Dan Lewis, Carol Glenzer, Karen Hafenstein, and most importantly my wife, Karen Ready, Nick and Melissa for their support on campus, support for leaving campus, support for getting on to other campuses and for allowing me to return home after traveling around. Thanks Yogi for keeping the last Karen happy in my absence.

During the past year I've had the opportunity to work with many northern California teachers throughout the K-12 range who've worked with me, written wonderful integrated lessons using and experimenting with Grammar Wars — and who have taught me a lot about the method, students, and testing. To Phil Good, Phil Finkel, the irrepressible Vonda Emmert, Claudia Reichle, Maryel Roberts, Patty Gunderson, Pam Blodgett for your work with Special Education kids, Cathy King, Jennifer Dobbs, Vicki Spotts, Robin Roberts, Molly Stimpel and Nikki Krey — thanks. To Mike Simmons at CSU Chico, thanks for the breakfast where you helped me distinguish using Grammar Wars for fact and concept instruction.

Special thanks to my partner in crime and comedy, Joe Bell and his development of the Standards "strands ladders" drafts he designed for this book. We've been working together in English and theatre one way or another since 1979. Joe, your support, professional passion and creative work on this project and for the various sections of this book are very appreciated. To quote my son, "You are the *man*!"

Contents

Introduction

Working with teachers throughout California at conferences and on-site trainings, I've had numerous conversations about how to effectively introduce and sustain the Grammar Wars method throughout the K-12 grades. The workshops generally start off with exercises that put teachers into the vulnerable, learning position of being students. Most, then, are rather nervous at some point, because the new skills, forcibly conducted at a fast speed to promote spontaneity, are practiced publicly.

Once the group of teachers is thirty to sixty minutes into the workshop process, we begin discussing their students and how the exercises might unfold in their classes. It's here that I found the content of *Grammar Wars: 179 games and improvs for learning language arts* doesn't give the answers to the questions most often asked by practitioners.

As a result, *Grammar Wars II: How to Integrate Improvisation and Language Arts* was designed to answer questions brought up by teachers. Besides new games, many of which were invented or inspired by teachers throughout northern California, there are more thorough explanations of several introductory games, along with lists of the productive and defensive behaviors that will show up. I tried to explain the behavioral goals that the exercises are supposed to produce. It is essential that instructors know what defensive behaviors will show up: the obviously negative ones and the subtle ones that only look like nice, polite behavior (you'll be surprised!).

For those who have been trained in performance skills, and those who haven't, there are aspects of improvisation that are uniquely weird. Because the work is done in empty space where you and your partners do not know initially where you are, where your sketch is going, and how it's going to end, it's a big risk. As a result, relationships between students (I call them actors from day one), and between the students and the teacher are critical, and in fact, are the only controllable elements in the process. Because of that important

1

aspect and the essential need to set a safe emotional platform, substantial time will be spent discussing a process and strategies for "inviting in" all the players.

If you are not a teacher but are reading this book (too much time on your hands?), you might skip over the sections in which we sound like educational practitioners, discussing how people learn. Over the past four or five years, working with hundreds of teachers around the nation and with employees in non-educational organizations in team-building and goal-setting workshops where I use improv as a strategy, I've been learning more and more about learning: how we do it, how we don't, and as a teacher how I can interfere with learning. I'll even give you tips on how to teach badly but get a great annual evaluation from your administrator. If you are an administrator, put this book down now!

Because this is a book with a goal to provide another effective method for teaching with the goal to produce observable, performance-based skills in you and your students, we will also talk about types of learning (memorization, understanding, and application) and measuring evidence of new learning. Now most of you who have been teaching will probably already know everything I'm going to say about testing or assessment in the pages to come; however, when I started seeing teaching, learning, and testing in the research I conducted with colleagues in northern California, many significant "ah-ha's" arrived at my metaphoric doorstep. So, because Grammar Wars can be done badly, and because we are teachers whose product is learning in our students, we need to know what measurements mean and how far along the learning process we are at any moment in the process.

The final important aspect of this text is the section on assemblies and workshops. Teachers asked, "Why Grammar Wars?" The title of the concept sounds like a battle or a competition, and ultimately, that is where a class or ensemble of actors can go with the improv skills and language arts knowledge they develop — public or in-class demonstrations. (I personally like the idea of students for back-to-school-night doing a Grammar Wars demonstration for, or in competition against, the parents to showcase their learning. I love to see the parents' faces when the students are, for instance, performing scenes requiring the alternating lines to be shifting syntax types. Everyone's having fun, the kids demonstrate learning the parents haven't grasped, and the parents look like foreign exchange students trying to understand an auctioneer.) So if you and your students like the content and process, the section on workshops and assemblies will give you some initial ideas on how to "show" or "travel" your skills. Take your students to work with students from a younger grade, and will your students ever feel like professional actors, and literate ones at that!

Learning can be quite impressive.

NOTE: The publishers felt it best to avoid any sexist connotation or the cumbersome use of "he/she." Therefore, we have adopted the singular use of the pronoun "they" in this book. According to many contemporary authorities, this is now acceptable English usage. *The Chicago Manual of Style, 14th Edition* states, "For the editor in search of guidance in avoiding sexist connotations the following sources are suggested: Casey Miller and Kate Swift, *The Handbook of Nonsexist Writing*, and Dennis Baron, *Grammar and Gender*. Along with these and other authorities, the University of Chicago Press recommends the revival of the singular use of 'they' and 'their,' citing, as do they, its venerable use by such writers as Addison, Austen, Chesterfield, Fielding, Ruskin, Scott, and Shakespeare."

Chapter 1
Background Issues

Tricking the World

As I've grown from delivering an activity-based to a standards-based curriculum in drama, the difference between the two has shocked me a bit and made me review the first fifteen years of my teaching career with embarrassed and humble eyes. The two are quite different, and I am sure that most of my colleagues have discovered the difference or already knew the two approaches and which was most effective.

Drama, especially improv, can be a lot of fun, and it is possible that some teachers believe that if students are having fun, they are learning. I question that. They might be learning another way to have fun, but the public contract with education is not to do what Saturday morning cartoons are designed to do to the general masses. Art instruction has suffered from the "frivolous" rap it often gets, even from educated elitists. I once worked in the arts-in-corrections system, teaching and directing workshops and productions (Hamlet got paroled before he could kill Claudius). One of my superiors in the program preferred that I direct shows and do traditional scene work rather than improv: I think she believed that improv is less disciplined, less of an art (and the reason most of the convicts were in the "joint" in the first place).

For the moment I'm going to agree with that insult of the dilettantes by saying that you can do Grammar Wars in your classroom, impress your colleagues and administrators, yet not be teaching your students much of anything, because (It's true!) improv exercises are fun activities. Kids will get involved, and it appears to be great classroom management.

Activity-based education says do the activity and they will learn. That might have some merit, but you can't guarantee what they'll learn. What you can guarantee is that all or most will do the activity. But that's it. It's like a soft reading program in school that assumes, "If the kids read more, they'll read better." Well, if they have bad habits and they practice more, they will reinforce or embed the bad habits by continued practice. Not clear yet? Try relationships. Possibly if a person suffers a divorce, he might have helped contaminate the relationship (despite any good intentions). Well, does that person get better by going in and out of a lot of new relationships, or might it be better to get some focused training on functional, *contributing* behaviors so that the next try will profit from quality skills and knowledge. I think learning in school is the same.

I can pretty much guarantee that you and your students will have a good time with improv games and exercises. I've only seen it fail once at a workshop in southern California at a Mentor Teacher Conference. There was one group of district or county administrators who tried to impress everyone by talking about the latest important developments from the state Department of Education. In their small group regardless of how I coached them, or how they heard the other groups in the workshop loosening up and "getting it," they only tried to impress each other. I don't know what was going on in their heads, but it had nothing to do with learning. (Note: I've had wonderful administrators repeatedly in my workshops so it's not endemic to that job arena.)

But having fun isn't necessarily learning. Grammar Wars is valuable if you approach the method as a tool to teach or reinforce drama or language knowledge, concepts and skills (in any content area actually). If your focus is to teach English/Language Arts, look for that always regardless of the noise in the classroom during the exercises and games. Be sure to read the sections "Opening Activities for Basic Skills," the Weave Method of lesson planning and "Testing for Learning."

Your administrator might walk in and think great learning and classroom management is occurring, but it is only the results from certain tests (your state or district assessments) or post-secondary writing that the parents and community want.

Performance Learning Isn't Desk Learning

I'm a total hypocrite. When I go to conferences or take classes, I prefer to sit in the back and never raise my hand, much less *do* anything. However, when I conduct workshops for students, teachers, or administrators, it's all active. Everybody (almost) will be forced to volunteer sooner or later. Of course, my concept of volunteering is different from what the dictionary might invite. Because I need people to demonstrate new learning with their bodies, voices and minds, they have to *do* things.

So I view every person with whom I work as having the fear factor that I have. Terrified is the assumed condition. Why? Because it's easier to sit in a chair or behind a desk and passively absorb information, rather than publicly demonstrate knowledge and concepts through skills.

Our kids know this and most of the time would prefer the teacher to talk (or whatever) and allow the students to sit and only pretend to listen and learn. There's far less risk sitting down.

Grammar Wars assumes skills and knowledge *presentation*, either in groups or solo. Sooner or sooner, everyone will have to get up and participate. So you can count on fear attending your classes, and the effective teacher will acknowledge and guide learning through the fear, so that the learning process is not paralyzed by the danger the students imagine.

My approach is not the nurturing mother style; rather, I initiate workshops and classes with assumptions and rules, some of which I've borrowed and some I've made up. Note that these are relationship factors rather than "acting" techniques.

Opening Assumptions:
- ✔ Your partner is intelligent.
- ✔ Your partner is creative.

Let's spend a moment here. There's no question in my mind that people are intelligent and creative. I don't know if for me this was an opening assumption or a conclusion, but I've seen it proved unendingly with students ranging from special education to valedictorians. I've seen it with adults ranging from convicted felons to organizational administrators. I've seen it in the paranoid and the confident.

What about you? Now you might be the shy type who has convinced yourself that "I'm not an actor. But over there, now there's someone who's good in front of people." There are lots of folk who might be like this or like you, if you find this characterizes your inner dialog. But I don't think it's true. I think you are very intelligent and very creative. Look how quickly you've come up with reasons not to perform. And I bet that if you were under pressure to come up with more reasons to not perform, you could do that quickly. Self-preservation is a super-charger for our personal engines.

Remember coming up with lies to your mother or father when you were a kid? Remember the excuses and lies you thought up when, because of speeding, you were pulled over on the roadside by a cop?

I think we show signs of incredible intelligence and creativity. Sometimes, however, I must admit, our morality or ethics might be a bit slow or underdeveloped, but that's not intelligence and creativity.

What's the point? Go back to relational physics. If your partners (spouse, colleagues, bosses, etc.) treated you constantly as though you were intelligent and creative, would you be willing to work or play with them? Remember, they would always be confirming that they believe you have and demonstrate both of those qualities. Would you be willing to work with them, try hard and come back for another round tomorrow? I imagine so.

Say I haven't been clear, and that's entirely possible. If I haven't made my point to you yet, reverse the assumptions about intelligence and creativity. Do you have a partner (spouse, colleague, boss, etc.) who constantly seems to convey to you that you are *not* intelligent and you are *not* creative? What's your attitude about working with them, about trying hard, taking risks or returning tomorrow for another round?

I tell my actors to consider these assumptions and to act as if they are true. I tell them that I will make sure that their partners do the same. Developing skills takes time, and if we don't make it safe to try, no one will show up tomorrow and learning will stop.

The Golden Rule always brings a smile to adults learning improv or Grammar Wars. I suppose that's partly because it doesn't seem like an obvious acting rule. It's really more like a moment from the Sermon on the Mount. Make Your Partner Look Good: at all costs, give to your partner; if you can set up your partner to succeed over yourself, do it; if your partner is suffering, save him or her, even if your action puts you at risk.

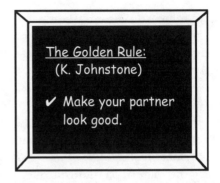

Remember relational physics: Make Your Partner Look Good and they will want to work with you again. And if you keep working together productively, learning will be constant and unending.

This section, therefore, is about fear in the classroom wherein you invite the students to leave the safety of their desks and try new things in front of others. There will be fear. However, if they are guided to be supportive and you support them into that new understanding and behavior, they will learn and find great joy in the process.

Treat them as you would want to be treated. It's a good rule of thumb.

Is It Really Competitive?

Improv actors are a weird crew. If you've ever seen TheatreSports™, then you have seen a competition that doesn't quite have all the same traits as your average sports competition. For instance, though there are two teams performing, scoring points, strutting without fretting on the stage, there is such good-natured fun about the whole thing that you might sense that there's more estrogen than testosterone on the stage. It's not unheard of for one team to be in the middle of a sketch when the opposing team, seeing a way to support and enhance the performers, might offer sound effects, backup singers or scenery items to help the opposing performers' sketch to be even more exciting.

When I coach an ensemble in classes without an audience, or in anticipation of performing for one, I encourage the entire class to see themselves as the real team, the troupe, the company. With that as the foundation, we create sub-teams from the whole, and the next session we remix so everybody works with everybody. Everybody plays with and against everybody. When our team does well, we applaud. When the other team does well, we lead the applause. When things bomb (I think it's somewhere between thirty and fifty percent of the time), we support the walking dead.

Regardless of whether I'm training actors in improv or organizations on team-building using improv, I push one assumption: concepts, programs, administrators come and go, but the one constant we live with is that we are in relationship with our partners. It's the foundation, the concrete, of our ensemble life. I believe that with that we have maybe three choices in that foundation relationship: we will work together, we will work despite each other or we will work against each other. It's a choice. It's an important choice. Given that scenes and life are unpredictable (the popular concept is "chaos"), our relationships determine whether or not we return to "play" the next day, whether or not we return to contribute fully or minimally, or whether or not we choose to leave forever.

To drive this idea home to adult groups, I ask them to size these ideas up to their work environment or their marriage. There's always this long silence that actually seems to have a weight. A heavy silence. All people are involved in less-than-ideal communities, large and small. And we all understand existing in a threatening relationship or group. They understand the idea of relational physics. Like gravity or the law of probability, in human relations you can count on some dynamics playing consistently. If you disrespect me long enough, either I won't play with you (I can refuse to work even if my body is still there), or I will become your servant. That means I won't create with you mutually; I will exist to praise your offers but I will never risk creating things myself. If you respect me and exist to "make me look good," however, I will return to work with you forever. With that last option, regardless of how bad my skills are initially, eventually I will improve and be good.

Value me: We will work productively forever. We will be a team.

Hurt me: One way or another, I will leave. You will end up alone.

Still not sure if it's true?

Look at your marriage.

Our relationships with our students are no different. We all have students whose bodies are in class, but they are not.

Is Grammar Wars really competitive?

Friends enjoy the game, the playing. Not the winning.

People who need to win, don't need to win. They desperately need losers.

Which Students Will Benefit?

During the 2000-01 school year I was involved in a research project with teachers throughout the K-12 in northern California. The focus was to train teachers at different grade levels at different schools on the Grammar Wars method while targeting specific English/Language Arts standards.

I got to work with mainstream and Special Education teachers, high school specialists and generalists at the primary and elementary levels. I was pleased to see that students across the spectrums enjoyed the active, kinesthetic approach, regardless of how close or distant the activities were to improvisational or traditional acting. More importantly, students in all categories showed learning.

Now for the differences. Performance opportunities re-categorize our students, quite outside of their more obvious social groups. I might have observed a group of "popular" athlete types at recess who comfortably strut, shout and confidently control the campus. However, some of these students in a classroom performance activity are virtually paralyzed with fear. Conversely, I've often seen students from fringe social groups or Special Education students who barely talk in public shine and succeed remarkably in the same Grammar Wars exercises. I teach AP English at my high school, working with what some consider to be the linguistic thoroughbreds of our school, students who are used to playing the education game successfully. It is not uncommon for these students to suffer disproportionately with games like these because the pace is too fast for them (they can't over-prepare to guarantee an "A"), and so they freeze up. But I have very academically average students who play with great comfort, at a fast pace, and outshine the school's elite.

Like all subjects and activities, Grammar Wars provides another tool by which we see the personal, academic and social skills of our students. It cuts across social and economic groups, across educational hierarchies and ages.

Our research showed that about ninety-eight percent of students like the approach (there were only two fifth grade girls at Meadow View School who "hated" it). While both boys and girls showed growth in learning, boys seemed to profit a bit more, especially the rowdy boys who hate sitting, reading and writing.

In your class, do you have students who are not engaged as you would like them to be? Here's another method that works. I think you'll be surprised to see who shines in the activities you use.

Pioneering Creativity

One of the strategies voiced by the Grammar Wars research team during the 2000-01 school year focused on the trail-blazing behavior of the teacher in leading the students into this creativity curriculum.

Demonstrate "play" yourself as you introduce skills and concepts, and as you demonstrate for the class, be the first to behave outside the "box." Tentative students cautiously glance around the room or the theatre as each gets involved in the new theatre exercises. Because the rules for behavior in a drama/improv workshop are different from the outside world ("conform and criticize"), new norms have to be set and modeled, and then they have to be accepted. Creative behavior has to be considered "safe."

When we look around any classroom, the homogenous or the heterogeneous, we see the norms of clothing, speech and behavior. All of us remember the desperate need to be accepted and to look like the crowd. In improv, or any theatre training, the task is to imitate life. The difference is that the school site and its social environment invite only a very small range of behavior: It presents one small choice of behaviors as if they were the only *correct* behaviors. Anything outside of the norm is usually labeled "stupid." Acting, and improv in particular, can call us to imitate *anything* in life: every possible emotion, every condition, every age, every intelligence, every life form, every natural event, realism, symbolism, etc., etc. Therefore, the behaviors that are socially condemned and dangerous to young people are the currency of performance.

So it helps set the stage for new behaviors and new norms if the teacher plays first. Have fun, animate, be the first to get on the ground, the first to sing, dance, cluck, cry, laugh, get a rash and scratch — whatever. And when you do it with energy and self-confidence, you tell the students that it's not only OK, it's quite fun — for all of us.

Be the first to play.

The Good News and the Good News

First, the good news.

The Grammar Wars method can be applied in forms that are very simple and safe (primary grades and introductory activities for new groups anywhere along the K-12 range). However, as confidence grows and the actors are more willing to risk and less interested in being "right" or "the winner," the exercises are constantly redesigned to push them to the fringe of the player's abilities. That quality puts challenge into all performances. After all, what fun would it be to see one or more actors doing something in which there was no challenge and no risk? Zippo! Boredom for everybody.

So the first good news is that it's too hard to do perfectly. Though exercises can be designed for 99.999 percent chance for success with the youngest players, with experience the activities get timed, or are layered with secondary tasks, or require an odd demonstration of some simple skill. All this stacking makes the task exciting and dangerous work, makes the actors brilliant when they succeed and makes the task's complexities at fault when the actors suffer.

Let me give you an example or two. Teachers tell me they know the alphabet, and for the most part when they tell me this, I let them think that I believe them. My false sincerity makes them feel safe (for the moment). I ask for two volunteers to come to the front of the room and recite the alphabet one letter at a time. I could have one come up and do the alphabet by herself, but that demonstration of the skill is the one they have mastered. So they courageously proceed through the twenty-six letters and feel pretty good when done. A safe start.

I then pull out a stopwatch and tell them that I'm going to time them. We begin and suddenly because it's timed, their alphabet has two "g"'s in it, "l" suddenly comes before "k," and the letters "w" and "x" have been removed completely. And they took fifteen seconds longer to accomplish the task! After another try, they adjust to that task and feel pretty smart, so I tell them we're going to do it one more time. They get set. I prep the stopwatch, pause, say, "Ready, set, *without vowels, GO!*" And again they swerve, dance, and stutter their way through, much to the delight of the audience. Good-natured, vulnerable heroes to the end, and the audience loves them for their humanity. (If this talk about vulnerable heroes doesn't make sense, hang on. It's a few pages downstream in this section.)

Let me restate the first good news: It's all too hard to do perfectly; therefore, errors are normal and all the actors make them. Enjoy the camaraderie!

Second, now the good news: you don't need any talent.

I'm pretty confident that there are a lot of people in theatre who would disagree with me here. They might cite times they've seen performances that were dismal because of an apparent lack of skill and inspiration on any one actor's part. I can't argue with them, so I won't.

But from a teaching point of view, I've had to grapple with the element of *talent* versus skill, and what to do about these two items as an instructor. I can't teach talent, but I can teach skill. All students regardless of the talent factor must have an equal chance at learning and demonstrating the knowledge and skills. In a fair world, can I evaluate all students on skills obtained by demonstration without regarding talent?

I think so. My experience is that if the skills are taught incrementally, slowly and clearly, all students can acquire and demonstrate skills. Now certainly talent will take some farther along, but I've seen the barely-endowed be very team-supportive and entertaining with basic skills. I think all can. I've seen it.

"But how can that be?"

Let's start off talking about comedy. Most people who resist performance, who think to be effective at improv one has to be funny, be animated, have a sense of humor, act "stupid," think comedy is an inspired talent. *I do* and *I don't. I do* because some people have a knack for it: they have genetic talent, or early on they got a few laughs at the table or in a classroom, liked it, and luckily stumbled into being able to repeat the behavior that got them that reward. *I don't* because I've seen people who have decided they're only good as an audience member, a responder to performance, be quite funny and contribute quite successfully simply because they adhere to technique.

14

Technique is teachable. Everyone can learn it. Ignorance and fear are the barriers. Of the two barriers, fear is the bigger obstacle and must be approached gently and strategically.

Spontaneity and accepting will make the audience smile and laugh.

I feel quite presumptuous pretending to speak with any authority on comedy. I mean, who am I? I teach acting and English in a town most people drive through and don't even have to try to forget. I work at a public school in an era when most people put the educational machine down as an archaic waste of taxpayers' money. I'm not smart enough to work at a college or university. So what are my credentials that I have anything to say?

I'm one of the guys who early on made my family laugh at the dinner table, in the car on vacations, at barbecues. I liked it, and I kept trying to do it more. It was fun and people liked it. I married a woman with a great sense of humor, who likes turning her colleagues into unsuspecting audiences. We talk about making people laugh and how to do it. We talk about "bombing" sometimes.

I direct shows at my school and work at making humorous situations pull laughs with various techniques, and then the actors and I talk about the comedy from night to night and audience to audience. I go to movies that are advertised as comedies and study what the actors are doing and what choices the directors made to play the humor. I buy books.

I do what all of us do when we're interested in something, and so along the way I've learned a little.

Comedy, to me, shows up in two major ways. This is a gross over-simplification. One, we surprisingly recognize ourselves on screen or on-stage in what we see or hear. (That doesn't sound very funny, does it?) Two, we receive a shock. If the shock infers a real danger or threat, we get scared; if the shock has no danger or threat, we can laugh or smile. (Did you ever really think that Wile E. Coyote wouldn't come back after crashing into the grill of a truck hauling atomic weapons?) Keith Johnstone says about comedy in *Impro for Storytellers*, "comedy treats painful things in a heartless manner" (p. 126). The heartlessness only occurs when we know that the danger is not real. That's why the final bit of a joke someone tells you is called a *punch* line: the first 90 percent is a set up that leads you to think or produce an interpretation going to the left, and the punch line snaps your thinking in the opposite direction. When we see a car accident, we get a "punch" from that shock, but only the most sadistic would be able to actually laugh.

Safe shock, you laugh. Dangerous shock, you freak out, call 911, whatever. Stupid shock, you hang out with other people.

"Why'd the chicken cross the road?" causes the audience to over-think the scene, so "to get to the other side" is surprisingly simple and obvious. You got tricked.

"I have a dog with no legs" possibly produces a pathetic image of the dog that causes the audience possibly to squirm or feel sad. The "punch" line, "every night I take him out for a drag," is surprising and almost cruel as the image of the dog skidding and rolling along on the sidewalk hits the audience's mind. If you know no dog is experiencing this, you "heartlessly" laugh. I know it's sort of sick, but I still find myself laughing at the image. The image is shocking, but I know the activity never really takes place, so there is no real danger. Wile E. Coyote. The Three Stooges.

Though the idea of shock is an element in both of the aspects of comedy, the latter (shock without threat or danger) is the primary trait of comedy that is important for this discussion of technique and the success of the "non-talented" (or at least those who protect themselves with this illusion).

Here's the skinny: when you are spontaneous and committed to your spontaneity, you will surprise/shock your audience. Period. The action sequences and conversations, if they are truly spontaneous (rather than what Keith Johnstone in *Impro for Storytellers* calls "clever" or "original," p. 142), will be surprising. As the actors accept and go with the spontaneous unfolding of events, the audience enjoys the plot. Please believe me that what I've said here is a simplified explanation, terribly over-simplified, but it's essentially true. Try some of the warm-up exercises here, attend an improv show, or watch an improv show on TV and see if what I've said doesn't bear itself out.

If you stick to technique, you will reap rewards.

Making Your Actors Into Heroes or
(The Actor Who Is Victimized by the Event,
Who Remains Goodwilled, Will Be the Hero)

Keith Johnstone, the creator of TheatreSports™, helped me to understand some important dynamics that occur between the actors and the audience. Even if you are a teacher and are simply exploring Grammar Wars, this is an important concept for your students' experience and for you to support. This idea will come up again in the section on warm-up games and offering and accepting.

Truth #1: Improv actors will be victimized by the game.

When we get up in front of the audience and either the audience or our spontaneous minds generate ideas we have to use in performance, success will seem impossible. The actors become victims.

Truth #2: Almost any character whom we follow on-stage long enough has the chance of capturing our goodwill, hopes or sympathies.

In traditional literature (books, TV, or movies), we are introduced to a lead character, follow him or her into a problem, watch them suffer, see them triumph, and enjoy their accomplishments as their life returns to peace. In post-modern narrative, we even see this occur to some extent with anti-heroes, characters with less-than-noble traits, simply by virtue of the time we have spent with them.

Truth #3: Goodwilled, benevolent victims are lovable and approachable.

If the hero we follow has virtuous traits, suffers through some vulnerability, we will want them to succeed (because we relate to their suffering). We will care for them. They are heroes.

If, however, they whine and complain, if they blame others, if they turn evil (not if they exact revenge), they no longer are heroes; rather, they become villains because they ruin our hopes for triumph and justice.

This is the case for stories in print and on the screen. This is also the case for improvisers in narrative work and Grammar Wars.

17

Truth #4: Grammar Warriors will be victimized by the game.

The games are too hard to do perfectly, because of the ideas offered by the audience or because of the structure of the task given. The actors are put in danger because that's what makes stories and performances interesting to watch. We are entertained by watching others suffer.

Review:

As we watch the actors, they become the lead characters, and we engage in their lives. Ultimately we project our concerns and desires onto them. We care about the outcome. If they *suffer well, try like mad, resist becoming defensive and blaming,* we love them.

Keith Johnstone said at a workshop at Stanford University that when improv is done well and the actors are goodwilled, suffer and succeed (or flop) with benevolence, the actual stage is the one place in the universe where everyone wants to be. I like that.

Think about it. A place where everyone supports everyone. A place where goodwilled people take on monumental tasks and risks, where they suffer, do the impossible, sometimes lose and sometimes succeed brilliantly, always with buoyant spirits. A place where we see the drama and the comedy of life. And when called up again, they show up as a team with vulnerability and vigor. Always ready to try.

My gosh. Who wouldn't want to trade in their seats to work in a place characterized by joy and resilient optimism!

Chapter 2
Basic Skills Sequence

Opening Activities for Basic Skills

This section is my effort to guide you through an opening set of exercises that have worked for me (by which I mean it's worked for students). Think in terms of students anywhere from eight years old to adult. I'll try to give you a sequence of activities and the rationale for each step and for the order. Just as, or more, important than the order is behavior to look for in the students. Regardless of whether or not the activities make them laugh or cry, the activities have a purpose in teaching them terms, concepts and skills in producing certain behaviors. Focus on that.

Because the learners are human, regardless of their willingness to play, they will end up sooner or later demonstrating defensive behaviors. I've seen it in myself, with amateurs and with professional actors in a master class with Keith Johnstone. We get defensive because we're human and we

> Offer: To suggest or create something by a verbal comment or a physical action.
>
> Accept: To use an offer made by a partner.

avoid risk. With each section when it's appropriate, I will also identify defensive behaviors that are clearly fear-based and destructive. I will point out behaviors that appear to be supportive but are deceptively self-protective. Selfishness disguised well.

Here are two indispensable terms I will use repeatedly. Tattoo them where no one can see but you.

Offer: To suggest or create something by a verbal comment or a physical action.

Verbal Offer: Two actors stand on an empty stage, and one says, "I can see that you've been rolling in the dirt again." The "offer" is dirt on the partner's pants and possibly that the partner is a young child.

Physical Offer: Two actors stand on an empty stage, and one mimes making a sandwich and handing it to the partner.

Accept: To use an offer made by a partner.

Verbal Accept: After A offers that B has dirt on his pants, B accepts by saying, "Yeah, I tripped running down the hill from the old abandoned mine."

Physical Accept: After A offers that B has dirt on his pants, B accepts by looking at his pants, looking shocked, and brushing the "dirt" off.

#1 What Are You Doing?

With groups that already know each other I start with "What are you doing?" It's silly, physical and quickly fun for the players. The skewed relationship between action and answer immediately dissolves "correctness" and makes everyone who is "wrong" right. At the outset, this activity declares that "here the rules are different."

Explanation: Two actors (A and B). A begins miming (offering) a familiar activity. B asks, "What are you doing?" A replies with an incorrect answer (a lie, if you will). A stops the first mimed action, and B begins miming (accepts) what A said (the lie). A then asks B, "What are you doing?" B lies, A does the second lie and the game continues.

Example:
A: (mimes bowling)
B: What are you doing?
A: Eating cereal (Stops "bowling")
B: (mimes eating cereal from a bowl)
A: What are you doing?
B: Trying to remove this Q-tip.
A: etc.

What to Look for/How to Coach

I want to see all participants having fun to start. If anyone looks as if they're suffering horribly, I will move over and offer encouragement, suggestions, and praise ideas (even if they have virtually no performance value) or actions.

I want to see every person using body, face and voice energetically sooner or later (energetically *accepting* the offer). I might state this goal to the group. I might stop this round of play and mention that I saw some groups working around the ground, some in a middle body level and some working as high as they can possibly reach. "Find activities that will get you into all three space areas." If some actors aren't animating much or are holding back energy, I might call out for them to come up with activities requiring different energy levels, different body parts, activities that use more space.

At the start of working with a new group, try to avoid identifying negative behavior. Offer alternatives that will invite variations and versatility. Resistant individuals may not warm up the first one or two times they play, but over several rounds or over a few days, they will come around if you make it safe and find ways to praise what little they are able to produce.

Once they get comfortable, give them themes to play with (i.e., Old West, things tall people live with, circus activities, Egyptian life, things people do in Reno during power outages, etc.). Or, make them use only active verbs. Or, make the answers use verbs that follow the alphabet (i.e., "I'm **A**sking for a raise," "I'm **B**elittling my hamster," "I'm **C**atching a butterfly," etc.).

Bottom line? A lot of energy, every body part in motion, laughter, bodies working in low, middle and high space. "Playing is *fun!*"

#1 What Are You Doing?

Skills	Defensive behaviors
✔ Using entire body ✔ Using face ✔ Using voice ✔ Working in different levels of space (high, medium, low)	✔ Standing and talking throughout the game ✔ Little animation ✔ Hand gestures only

#2 Yes, and ...

If I'm working with an eclectic group that doesn't know each other, I prefer to start off with "Yes, and ... " because it's safer physically and lets people explore spontaneity with words, bodies passively sitting in chairs in a circle. Emotional safety first.

Explanation: Four to five people (no more and no less) sit in chairs in a circle facing in, relatively tight. (This helps hearing each other if there are a lot of groups because the noise level in a room really goes up.) Facilitator offers a subject to the groups. One person in each group is to begin talking about the subject offered. The talker must talk constantly until interrupted by a group member. All interrupts must begin with "Yes, and ... " When B interrupts A, A must stop talking immediately. B talks until interrupted, etc.

Note: The size of the group is important. If the actors are learning the game for the first time, groups smaller than four put too much pressure on the novices. If there are too many members, it's easy for people to hide, escaping any pressure to support the activity at all. Stick with four to five.

Example:

Facilitator: Your activity begins with commercial products for domestic rodents.

A: I just came back from Rats 'R Us and got a great deal on a hamster swing set. The lady at the counter said that she just bought one for her son, and he hasn't stopped playing with it.

B: Yes, *and* I must live by her and her son because yesterday as I was leaving my house, Billy Watters, the kid who lives four houses down was swinging on a miniature swing set, one leg each through two different swings.

C: Yes, *and* I know Billy Watters!!! Do you mean the kid who ...
Etc.

What to Look for/How to Coach

After playing this game over several rounds, I want to see actors comfortably interrupting each other with ideas that tie back to the lines that were just spoken: that's evidence of listening. Also, I want to see every group member interrupt and offer content proportionally. Speakers should talk consistently, without long or unjustified pauses, even if they are not sure of the very next word coming out of their mouths. Hopefully there is a sincere and emotional tone in the delivery that makes the content seem honest. Interruptions should come at the end of thoughts, unless the speaker is clearly in pain/fear. If the speaker is giving signs of horrible tension, the partners should interrupt immediately to "save" the panicking partner. With practice, a well-functioning group might, with the tenth interruption, also re-include specifics from one of the earliest offers. (This technique is called "reincorporation" and in this case is a true compliment to whomever offered that specific item earlier!)

The Wisdom of the Title: "Yes, and ... "

After playing the game, with the participants having had a chance to develop some of the productive behaviors and laugh together, I talk about the value of the words in the title. I do this with acting workshops and when I conduct workshops in organization development.

Think about the predictable effect of working in a group where no matter what you offer, on your good days or bad, your partners will say, "Yes" to what you've contributed. I think back to meetings I've been in where I've had thoughts that made sense to me, but I kept it all to myself either because I wasn't feeling self-confident, or I thought someone would ridicule my idea (and so ridicule *me*). But if my partners were trained to find the value in my contributions, to say "Yes" to what I thought *(Remember: My partners begin from the assumption that I am creative and intelligent!)*, might I continue to participate regardless of how I am feeling? Might I feel more like a valued member of the team? Would your behavior in any group (family, school, church, club) change if your value were constantly being affirmed?

But we don't stop there. The title is "Yes, and ... " The word "and" takes the value even higher. Not only did what you say deserve a "yes," the idea was so good that I want to continue talking about what you brought up. I want to be a part of your idea; it's that good.

When people value me, I want to contribute (work, play, give, support). Even if today doesn't go so well, I will return to that supportive group tomorrow to try again. It's not the success of the activity from which I get the pay-off; it's the quality of the relationship that brings me back for more.

Defensive Behaviors and Corrective Techniques

Tell the Truth

Defensive behaviors will show up because we are human. Listen for "Yes, and but ... " or "Yes, but ... " If it shows up, between rounds, point it out and ask why someone said it. Generally, people will come up with something like, "Well, I didn't agree with her." It's curious that in the instructions I never said anything about tell the truth, debate the facts, whatever. Sometimes, one non-participant will say, "I didn't talk because I didn't know anything about the subject." Tell them that knowledgeable, truthful responses were never a part of the instructions. *Making your partner look good*, however, was an important operating rule. If your partner is tired of doing more than his share, but you don't help because you'd *have to be creative*, your team may not see you as much of a team player. The instinct to speak truthfully, not creatively, to be "right" or honest to my life and thoughts rather than to be creative, playful and supportive of my partner, overrides the rules and instructions given at the outset. Review the rules with them, side-coach during the round to have them avoid silence and their "Yes, but" interrupts. Ask them, "What does 'yes' mean? What does 'but' mean? What does the 'but' do to the 'yes'?"

Relational Physics: If you disagree, devalue or contradict me enough, eventually I will leave, stay but not play, or stay and seek revenge.

Silence

It is somewhat common for someone not to play at all during the first rounds of "Yes, and ... " That's fine. The next game in the sequence will take care of that. A non-participant will, however, frustrate some new actors enough that after one round is over, the talking actors will either say within the group or to me in front of the entire group, "Robin didn't say a thing the whole time." Though that might be true, I assume that Robin didn't play because Robin was frightened to death. Certainly, pointing out to a crowd that she didn't talk does not support or encourage her, doesn't *make your partner look good* and isn't going to ensure that she'll come back tomorrow to try again. The comment does try to relieve one frustrated actor's feelings at the expense of another. I will review the criticism in light of the operating principle (Make Your Partner Look Good), point out that such a comment doesn't meet that principle, and highlight that new games have unfamiliar rules and that makes people wary. Caution is a normal and sometimes healthy response.

Laughing

If you see anyone laughing "uncontrollably," you might point it out in some safe way that that might be (it *is*) a cop out. It essentially says, "You are so funny, I love listening to you and I'm laughing so hard that I can't even think." I've seen people laugh this way even while the talker is sending various signals that she wants to be interrupted (saved) so someone else can work under the pressure. The laughter looks like a compliment, but it's deceptively selfish.

Accepting an Old Offer

Listen to the interrupts as you walk around to the groups. Is the new interrupt building upon what was just said, or is it building upon what was said two or three speakers ago? All interrupts must reflect what was *just* said. If your brain had something, but the group moved on, drop your thought and move with the new speaker. Point this out nicely if you see it show up. They will complain that they "can't think fast enough." They can. They will. Right now they are just trying to sound right, intelligent, or are trying to know what they are going to say before the words start coming out (sound reasonably intelligent). This is self-interest competing against *making your partner look good.*

#2 Yes, and ...

Skills	Defensive behaviors
✔ Giving and taking focus ✔ Speaking spontaneously ✔ Talk until interrupted ✔ Interrupt partners at the end of thoughts (Don't interrupt after only two words) ✔ Interrupt if your partner gives signals of stress ✔ New comments build upon the content of the person who was just interrupted (not what was said two or three comments ago) ✔ Listen to your partner and the specifics of the offer ✔ Speaking confidently as if it all made sense and were true	✔ Someone says, "Yes, but ... " or "yes, and but ... " ✔ Closing down body language ✔ Laughter at what the talker is saying, suggesting that "This is so funny, I'm in a spasm and cannot even think." ✔ Interrupting, but to build upon what was said one or two people ago ✔ Only answering with real content ("I know nothing about this subject, so I have nothing to say.") ✔ Watching the talker give "help me" signals, the partners say nothing, preferring to let the talker squirm and suffer

#3 Q and A

This is an excellent game to do following "Yes, and ... " especially when you introduce these exercises for the first time. It is not uncommon for one new actor not to offer anything during "Yes, and ... ."

That's OK. "Yes, and ... " requires the interrupter to take the initiative. But if the actors are afraid, uncertain or frozen, there's no way they will interrupt and turn the spotlight on themselves.

"Q and A" offers an easy solution. With this game the shifts for another actor to speak are forced on the next actor; we don't wait for someone to be benevolent. Now the opportunity to speak is somewhat "forced" on the quieter actors.

Explanation: This game is like Hot Potato. (Remember that game?) Groups of four or five sit in circles, separately so the noise factor from one group doesn't interfere with the communication in another group. One actor looks at another and asks a simple question. That action *throws* the metaphoric potato to the next member. This second member *catches* the potato by answering the question with a one-sentence answer. Now because the potato is hot, the task is to turn and fire another question to another team member quickly to avoid getting *burned*. So that's the cycle that repeats: ask, answer, ask, answer, ask, etc.

Simple, huh?

Example:

A: How's your day been? (to B)

B: I just got over my cold. Did the mail arrive? (to C)

C: I saw a package leaning against the post outside. Do all packages "tick"? (to B)

B: I wasn't listening. Could you repeat that? (to A)

Etc.

What to Look for/How to Coach

After playing "Yes, and ... ," students will get into this quickly. Though it is very similar to the game "Yes, and ..., " in many ways it is the complete opposite. The former is "fast" for the speaker; "Q and A" works at a quick pace for everyone. The goal behaviors are a willingness to ask and be asked: energy and pace in the exchanges. Though most people are capable of having quick, short-exchange conversations on topics in which they are interested, the artificial nature of this exercise makes them act as if they know none of the key question words (who, what, when, where, why — plus can, did, could, would, has, etc.). Tell them the key question words or write them on the board so they can refer to them.

Saving a Partner with Brain Freeze

The spoken lines in "Q and A" are short (we hope) and quick like net play in a doubles tournament in tennis. Nonetheless, actors will get halfway into a question and freeze up. Because good improvisers are there to "make their partners look good," they will interrupt the act of a brain-dead partner *as if the question were completely and intelligently asked* in order to take the focus (save the partner). Though the question may not have made sense (yet), treating it as complete and answering it does several remarkable things: it saves the brain-dead actor (friend for life), makes the interrupter look benevolent (likeable hero type), introduces an exchange that has never been heard before (fresh work), creates an "impossible" that the goodwilled actor solves and thereby looks brilliant to the audience. What a payoff for everyone!

I want to see all actors speaking quickly and with some presentative tone that's in the body, face and voice. Initially, I might coach them for simple confidence in their demeanor, because if their pace is up, they will be saying some surprising things that undermine their security and confidence — so the appearance of confidence is a nice mask. (The audience knows they feel insecure inside and enjoys the tension and pretense.)

Patterns

Some groups develop unspoken contracts for mutual security. After a moment they have developed the pattern of playing "Q and A" taking turns by going in a clockwise or counter-clockwise pattern. They do this despite the fact that the instructions and demonstration described a random ordering. Why? The pattern politely gives each student "time off" to relax and watch. In contrast, if it's random, then anyone might have to answer and ask at any moment. Surprise! Less risk with a predictable pattern. If you see it in any of the groups, coach them away from that security blanket.

Right from the start you will see several traits in the answers that we need to spot and coach away, one at a time.

Defensive Answers and Corrective Techniques

Planning Answers (Not Listening)

"Clever" actors will plan a statement/answer to a question prior to the question even being asked. When they are asked (the potato thrown), they quickly respond and it looks like quality spontaneity; however, if you hang around to watch the actor field the next exchange and the answer is totally unrelated, and they have a self-satisfied little grin, you might be witnessing a defensive behavior that you'll want to address. Now that I've said that, ironically, sometimes a truly spontaneous response might not be related to the question at all, and at the outset that's a good sign. How can you tell the difference? Look at the eyes of the actor. A grin suggests, "I'm delightful"; a wide-eyed look that says, "Where'd that come from?" suggests the actor was honestly and vulnerably open to the first thought to show up. That's a goal behavior for the moment.

Ricochet Questions

Nervous actors will commonly take the question asked of them, turn and ask the same question (in some form) of the next actor. Here's an example:

A: Do you like dogs? (to B)
B: Yes. Do you (like dogs)? (to C)
C: Yes. D'you? (to A)
Etc.

I call that a ricochet question and it's defensive because it bypasses original creation. I'll just take your used stuff and throw it to the next guy rather than risking coming up with my own and possibly saying something ridiculous. It's also boring from a standpoint of varying or developing imagery. (I'll talk about that later.) Here you might make available the list of question words from which they might choose to assist their creation of new questions.

"No."

It's really weird how this behavior, which Johnstone calls "blocking," is so predictable. The first time you have a group play this game, the vast majority of responses will be negative. Even if the questions are simple and mundane, new actors opt for "no." It's like verbal karate: deflect anything and everything that's coming at you. "No" does that. Require all answers to be positive. (Initially, that means, say "yes.") "Yes" is better than "no," but there's an even better technique still.

Accept and Offer in the Answer (Building Imagery)

There are two stages of positive, *accepting* answers: the first is to simply say "yes," and the second is to accept the offer and to offer additional elements to the offer in your response. Let me give an example:

Good Positive Accept:
    A: Have you owned that Rolex long? (Offer)
    B: Yes, I have. (Positive, limited Accept)
Better Positive Accept:
    A: Have you owned that Rolex long? (Offer)
    B: This one was a gift from my dad on my fifth birthday. (Positive Accept with new content)

The simple "yes" response, though positive, is passive (called "wimping"). It says, "You create stuff and I'll just sit back and use your stuff. That way I don't have to risk. If the sketch flops, it's your fault because you created everything."

Developing Imagery

This is simple and effective. Watch what happens when you require your students to accept with an offer (essence of "Yes, and … "). They will laugh more and build energy. Why? Each offer produces imagery in the group. If I offer, "Hey, have you owned a dog like that since I've known you?" I am putting in the audience's minds two friends, some odd-looking dog, possibly an outdoor or a living room picture, etc. If the partner simply says, "Yes," nothing new is added. But if the partner accepts with, "Let me show you the weird box I found him in. Someone stuffed him into my brand new mailbox," now we have developed the details in everyone's minds, some curiosity about a unique box, the mystery of where it came from (a mystery for the actors, too, since they have no idea about how to solve the mystery they've created), and a new mailbox that might clarify the imagery of a man with his own house (not an apartment). The story is ready to start unfolding. That has resulted from the better Accept. Now if both actors continue the accepting and offering, the story takes off and the audience has a chance of getting engaged in it.

#3 Q and A

Skills	Defensive behaviors
✔ Giving and taking focus	✔ Answering questions with "no"
✔ Spontaneity	✔ Answering with a prepared
✔ Knowing key question	answer planned prior to the
words (who, what, when,	question being asked
can, did, etc.)	✔ Thinking of "good" questions
✔ Interrupting half-asked	✔ Rotating in a circle or some
questions, as if the question	other predictable pattern
were finished, if the speaker	✔ Thinking of accurate answers
is stumbling and suffering	✔ Silence
✔ Speaking confidently as if it	✔ Body language that says,
all made sense and were true	"Don't ask me anything"
✔ Quick rather than slow	✔ Negative answers
answers because slow	✔ "Yes" answers that do not add
means they are looking	to the images of the question
for a real answer	✔ Giving ricochet questions
✔ New questions constantly	(someone else's question
✔ Every answer accepts and	with only one or two words
then offers on the content	different)
of the question asked	✔ Repeating the same question
✔ No negative answers (ever!)	word for two or more
	questions (i.e., "do," "can," etc.)

#4 Word-at-a-Time (Used in Professor Know-It-All)

I use this game to point out to actors and employees the brain's natural action of trying to predict the future for security's sake. As sentences are formed and each actor gives up the majority of control of the process, each can almost sit back and watch their brain anticipate where the sentence is going to go. Johnstone calls that "living in the future." For improv, however, it's better to live in the now.

Explanation: Two or more actors sit in a circle. This activity does go, by agreement, in a predictable pattern (clockwise or counter-clockwise). One person starts the first sentence with only a single word. The second offers the next word in a developing sentence, the third offers a third, and around and around it goes, sentence after sentence — and the story unfolds.

Example:

A: Once
B: upon
C: a
D: time
A: there
B: was
C: a
Etc.

What to Look for/How to Coach

Listening

I want to see partners listening and speaking clearly with volume. Not listening insults the value of the speaking partners and screws up the grammar. Speaking clearly with sufficient volume is good technique which allows all partners to get all the important information so they can offer well.

Pace

Speed of response is a good thing, even if it sometimes screws up the grammar or meaning. Cautious, correct-mindedness slows down the pace and dissolves the performance value of the event.

Predicting the Sentence

If an actor tries to predict the future of the sentence and thereby prepare an acceptable word to insert, problems can occur. Here's the main error: if I try to anticipate how the sentence will form so I can pre-plan a word, it is more than likely that the partner preceding me will throw in his own word that isn't a part of my planned sentence. As a result, I do a sequence of things that takes time and generates panic: I go into a little shock that my word doesn't work now, I get a little mad at my partner for not imagining what I imagined privately, I have to regenerate the original sentence in my head having abandoned my original word choice and then I have to come up with a new word to insert. My, my what a busy head I have now!

The alternative is to train your head to just listen (stay in the *now*), and to trust that you are intelligent and creative: your brain will come up with something if you just listen to the sentence as your team creates it.

Clever and Original Answers

Clever answers are usually followed by the smirk of self-congratulation. Beginning actors will accomplish some trick of humor by throwing in elephants, hippopotamuses, pink or purple things, and other cliché absurdities. Initially, these offers will get a snicker because they do shock, but they have the narrative productivity of tripping a friend as she walks down the aisle between rows of desks. It's funny once for the immature, but then you develop a reputation for being stuck developmentally. The laughter dies.

Side note: I don't know where this coaching tip fits in so this is as good as anywhere. Young actors (and older) when nervous will automatically respond to their nervousness by throwing in offers about flatulence, burps, getting drunk, gay bars, B.O., puke and swear words. Because of their shock value, they do give pay-offs to the perpetrators. After a while, though, the value goes away and we just have a repetitive, uninteresting loop of content. Boring. I've seen this done with dysfunctional adolescents and with the most pious of churchgoers. When we get nervous and operate at spontaneity, anything in our lexicon can come out; and it probably will. If you let me think before I speak, I will control those eruptions.

I don't freak out if someone says something off-color — initially. I will, however, point out that we all know those words and things get laughs because of shock, but eventually they will lose their value. And if we trust our intelligence and creativity, we will come up with a thousand and one other, fresh things that will continue to make our work new, lively, and interesting.

That's usually enough to allow us to move forward.

#4 Word-at-a-Time

Skills	Defensive behaviors
✔ Listen to the sentence as it unfolds ✔ Live in the "now." Don't plan where the sentence will be when it's your turn ✔ Spontaneity ✔ Sustaining the grammar of the sentences ✔ Speaking clearly for your partners and the audience	✔ Clever answers (you can see this in their eyes and smile when they think they're witty) ✔ Planning for their turn to give a "good" answer ✔ Mumbling ✔ Body language is withdrawn ✔ Looking at the preceding actor with a negative glance as if to say, "You offered the wrong word" ✔ Correcting any of the partners

C.R.O.W.E.

The cornerstone of scene work for improvisers is buried in this acronym: C.R.O.W.E. It stands for character, relationship, objective, where and emotion/condition. In Belt and Stockley's book, *Acting Through Improv: Improvisation Through TheatreSports*, discusses this tool. The C.R.O.W.E. is to an improviser what the 5W's (who, what, when, where, why) are to a method actor. Each tool is the template for the essential requirements for a scene. Why? Because each tool is an essential combination of elements from real life, and in acting, we look to imitate.

The "C" stands for character. The characters have ages, genders, physical appearances, physical and vocal traits (how they move and speak), energy levels, reaction patterns, physical and vocal mannerisms, intellectual speed, morals, ethics, etc. This element of every scene is important, because characters determine events and events reveal and shape character.

The "R" represents relationships. This focuses on the character's interactions and attitudes towards others, present and mentioned in spoken lines. Relationship is essential, because it affects our behavior in real life and therefore, on stage.

"O" focuses our attention on what I see as the "motor" in all scenes. It stands for objective, what the method actors call "intention" (I've never liked that word choice). In real life we are constantly motivated by our desires (overlaps with character and relationships, doesn't it?). If that's not clear, let me try this comparison with you. Have you ever watched a sporting event, professional or amateur? I see this with adolescents and little athletes. Have you seen them stand out in left field, checking the height of the grass? Or maybe a football player on the defensive line who pretends to slam into the offensive opponent (but really sends the signal that he doesn't want to get hurt!). I know that guy; that's how I played for quite a while (then quit). The lack of interest and drive dissolves the intensity of the event. Now flip it. Think of any time you saw someone doing something with intense interest, whatever it was. That intensity draws our interest. Eyes locked on an obstacle or person who can serve my interests, or who is in my way so I must destroy them! The actor who goes after a goal with sincerity and intensity makes scenes move with interest.

The "W" is the where, the location for the scene, and beginning actors often miss this asset. I have divided the where into two elements. Number one, *things* are everywhere when you choose a location, so imagine what things would, could and should be there. Besides being rather obvious, why is that so important? Beginning improvisers think that if they simply talk, they will be acting and the audience will be interested. (In fact, I don't think beginning actors really think about the audience; they are self-absorbed and self-protective 99.9 percent of the time.) Without a physical environment, we end up having to watch a "talking head" scene. These scenes are tedious for the viewers and safe for the beginning actor. If before, during or immediately after the first verbal offers, the actors define and start using the objects in the environment, we will have a three-dimensional scene. That's good for the actors because they will have things to do (imitate real people's actions and lives) and for the audience because they will have things to imagine that make the scene richer. There's a bonus, too. Improv actors have to jump without caution into the uncertain future of their scenes. If you let your imagination design the specifics of the where, those things in the environment are then tools you can use during the beginning, middle and end of the scene. The things will give you ideas and help when you need to create problems to advance the narrative and solutions to save the hero.

The other where item that is an element of life, which affects human behavior *(and remember! The job of actors is to imitate life)*, is the human/actor's *relationship to the location*. The quick version goes this way. Locations are like characters: we react to them. In some places we are comfortable, and in others we are not. That affects our behavior. Take two living rooms. Same design, furniture, knick-knacks, same paint. Walk in and the question for the actor is, how will you behave? Will you stand frozen or will you sit? If you sit, how will you sit? Sprawl? Knees and feet together and hands on thighs sitting rigidly upright like a two-by-four board? Well, if it's the living room at my house where I've lived with my family and our "stuff," I might toss my things on the floor and flop on the sofa, feet on the coffee table. If, however, I'm a teenage boy and it's the living room at my new girlfriend's house, I've never been here before, and her father might be home, I might remain only on the fringe of the room, leery of even stepping into the space. Point: My relationship to the place affects my behavior, so as an actor I must design with this real-life element.

The final letter is "E." Belt and Stockley don't have the "E" in their C.R.O.W. I don't think I invented it, but you won't find it in their book *Acting Through Improv*. At any moment in our lives, our bodies, minds or emotions drape us in emotional states, moods or conditions (i.e., *happy, quiet* and *freezing*, respectively). What are you feeling right now as you're reading this book? Angry that you bought it? Content because your dog's asleep? In agony because you just got a paper cut? Whatever, there's some metaphoric weather that's making your day, affecting your experience of it; therefore, the actor must build that into his or her scene work.

#5 Corridors (Belt and Stockley, page 107)

Corridors is a scene-starting game and a reasonable exercise to do after doing the earlier described exercises and concepts. The actors have offered and accepted, the concept of C.R.O.W.E. has been explained to them, and now they can begin scenes with more complete offers.

Explanation: Make two rows, each with an equal number of actors, facing in towards the other row, as if you are about to do the Virginia Reel. Each actor in Row A has her partner directly across in Row B.

Here's what the pairs of actor will do: The first actor (A) steps halfway into the "corridor." Using mime and spoken words, the actor will make a full C.R.O.W.E. offer and then hold for her partner in Row B to step into the corridor and mime and/or speak to accept the context of the first offer. When actor B is done with the accepting response, actor A says "Thank you," and the scene is over. Remember, "Corridors" is just a scene-starting game. The two actors step back into their original rows and the next pair goes, A offering and B accepting. You do that in a zipper fashion from one end to the other. Then go back to the original end and repeat only with B offering, A accepting and B ending with "Thank you."

Coaching Tips

Demonstrate an example first because when you explain the C.R.O.W.E. concept to them initially, and then tell them that each will need to come up with a full C.R.O.W.E. offer to convey, each will feel a bit overwhelmed. (It would be the same if you took a juggling class and the professional told you, "We're going to start off juggling three balls at once!" You'd look around for your car keys and run.)

I ask the class after my example to come up with their own complete offer. Some balk and have that "deer in headlights" look. Over time I've developed this little formula that serves the nervous needs of most of the new actors.

1. Think of a specific place (Taxi cab, not Paris — Paris is too general to lock specific things and a specific objective and relationship).
2. What two people might be there?
3. What might one of the people say to the other that would make the C.R.O.W.E. clear to the other? (Making the partner step into the scene easily, which makes the accepting *partner look good*.)

Let me make up an example now to illustrate:

1. Specific place: In a section of the woods with a lot of tall pine and oak trees.
2. Two people: Two loggers.
3. Thorough offer:

> Actor A: "Larry, this is what 'old growth' forests look like (pulls out a map from back pocket). If we head just over that ridge, I'll show you the area we're allowed to mark and cut. You drive this time." (Cross and mime getting into opposite sides of a truck.)

Were all the C.R.O.W.E. elements there?

Item	Actor A	Actor B Options
Character	Adult logger of the speaker's gender. Methodical, patient, considerate. Age anywhere between 25 and 60.	Eager to learn, or nervous at the task, or overbearing, etc. Possibly younger than the trainer. Gender of the actor.
Relationship	Trainer	Trainee
Objective	To train the employee well so that they feel confident and able	To learn the trade? To impress the trainer? To find secret patches of illegal marijuana? To work out in the remote woods to avoid the FBI?
Where	The woods where he's comfortable	Woods where he's comfortable? Or nervous?
Emotion/ condition	Calm, content	Eager? Nervous?

You get the idea? If the actor I'm training still can't generate a C.R.O.W.E. offer, I ask another actor standing by to give the uncertain actor an idea.

There are a ton of things that will surface as you start to play. If you know what to look for and facilitate it well, you will get a lot of instruction through samples of good and bad technique.

Look for These:

1. Beginning actors forget to give a where.
2. They say the C.R.O.W.E. with their lines but don't sound the way a character would naturally speak.
3. They almost never convey all the C.R.O.W.E. items.
4. Most will talk without doing much physical action (physical offers).
5. Many will accept as minimally as possible.
6. Some will be given very specific offers but will ignore them.
7. Some block.
8. Some people mumble, talk too fast or mime badly.
9. Some offers aren't clear and the partner will freeze.
10. Some offers are vague and the partner boldly accepts differently than the offering actor intended.
11. Some don't step into the corridor.

1. Beginning actors forget to give a where.

Why? I have no idea. When it happens (you get a "talking head" scene), ask them, "If you were to change the offer to make the where clear to your partner and the audience, what would you say or do?" They'll come up with something. Ask all the other actors about to go to review their offers before you continue the exercise to make sure each does or says something to make the where clear. You might require them from now on to *do something physical* with the items in the location within the first offer.

2. They say the C.R.O.W.E. with their lines but don't sound the way a character would naturally speak.

Some will do this to get a gag laugh; it's like mocking the rules of the exercise. Here's an example:

Actor A: "Since I'm a police officer pulling you over on the highway,
I want to give you a ticket because I'm grouchy."

Police officers do not speak this way (if one does, just take the ticket
and drive off) in realistic, day-to-day operations. Most of us might
expect, "License and registration, please." That would be more realistic.
Shoot for normal realism. The goal is to offer to get scenes going so that
the partner and audience know what's going on. If the partner feels as
though the offer is clear, he will be able to join comfortably and that
actor will like working with the one who offered well.

3. They almost never convey all the C.R.O.W.E. items.

Conveying Characters

Beginners might just use their own voice, body, or emotion/
condition instead of creating an all-new character. This is the novice
actor who only recites lines rather than conveys scene elements with
the actors' tools. Encourage the actors to animate body, face or voice
with something fitting their offer, not arising from their normal traits.

Conveying Relationship and Objective

Most will tend to give something for the relationship and objective
though it may not be dynamic or play well to the seats at the back of
the house. Young students will tend to go with negative relationships or
ones that require a neutral tone (indifferent or harmless stranger). These
are safer to do and keep them at a distance from having to change or
be vulnerable. Coach them to positive relationships, or invite alternative
lines that build relationships that "come together" in some way.

The characters of the early C.R.O.W.E. efforts will probably have
objectives, but they may be expressed only with words. Invite
physical actions and possibly the use of vocal or facial tones to achieve
their goals. Initially, we're looking for the young actors to use their
bodies, faces and voices intentionally and with energy.

Conveying Emotion or Condition

I've already talked about the where not showing up too much, so
let me go to the last item, emotion/condition. This element is a filter that
separates the goats from the sheep in beginning actors. Nervous actors
never stray too far from showing that they're nervous, no matter what

they think they're conveying onstage. The enthusiastic ones, however, will try a variety of emotional tones and conditions immediately with games like "Corridors." As you run the game, in each scene look for the C.R.O.W.E. elements and point out the wealthy and the lean exchanges so the actors develop their creative abilities and their critical eyes.

4. Most will talk without doing much physical action.

To the nervous and tentative, saying something without moving, just "filling" space avoids risk and is therefore safe, so many will do these talking head scenes. For the first phase maybe allowing them to do something and survive is acceptable. But once they find that they can offer and accept and get off stage alive, push them to get physically involved. When they see their peers physically offer and thereby set the physical location so much more richly, they'll want to do it, too.

As you coach them, you might do a round or two of "Corridors" over a few days or workshops with the restriction that all opening offers must convey the C.R.O.W.E. without using any words or mouthed words. Make the mime convey as much as possible. They'll do it effectively.

5. Many will accept as minimally as possible.

This is the fear thing, along with the "I don't know what to do!" excuse of the paranoid. Some of the fearful beginners are approached with a knock on their "door" and a question whether or not they'd like to test out this new vacuum, yet they forget to open the door and use only part of their wrist and two fingers of their right hand to reach for the vacuum. I ask, "What else might you have done," to which they say, "I don't know." I ask if there was a door and if it would be fitting to open it before replying and reaching for the product. They get the idea, and everyone sees how nerves and self-consciousness override the simple, honest actions that we all instinctively perform in real life.

Encourage actors to identify the location offered, quickly imagine objects in that place, and use or refer to them. All this will help the audience see. The honest work is impressive and the other actors will get it quickly. Reluctant actors will learn to make the location and the other C.R.O.W.E. elements a rich and varied part of their scene work.

6. Some will be given very specific offers but will ignore them.

Go back to the traffic stop example from a bit earlier. The offering actor mimes getting off the motorcycle, hooks his hands on the equipment belt, walks up to the window (waist high) and knocks. He stoops over a bit to look at the level of a sitting driver. The partner, *still standing*, maybe mimes winding down a car window, and says, "It's in the glove compartment." The whole time he's *still standing* though the first actor is bent over to offer a sedan-level car. The first actor made a physical offer (without words he offered the car level and a sitting driver) and the second actor didn't see or accept the physical offer).

Coach the actors to listen with their ears *and* eyes. Offers come in all shapes and sizes. Again, requiring the team to play "Corridors" without any spoken words will train the actors to look for different clues to read and use their bodies to offer and accept.

7. Some block.

Blocking is not accepting offers. An actor might block by saying, "No" or by de-creating, or re-creating a partner's offer. "No" is a sin in improv because it's one form of a status move: your "No" says, "Your idea stinks. You are not intelligent or creative." Do that enough with an acting partner (or anyone with whom you are in a relationship), and you will sooner or later reap the benefits of your constant devaluing. (Not clear? Ask your union's president. Ask your spouse.) Coach your actors to always say "yes."

De-creating is a form of blocking where one actor offers, say, a wallet ("Is this your wallet you dropped?"). The partner looks at the extended hand and says, "There's nothing in your hand." This is a type of "no" answer ("I won't play with you"), but the response really erases the object that was offered into the scene. Early on, this behavior will get a laugh because of the status play (insult humor), but like the maturity level of middle school students, it's funny for a short time in the world of the insecure; however, before too long people see it for what it is and stay away from the perpetrators. Block enough, and you block alone.

Re-creating occurs when an offer is made and the second actor re-creates the element offered.

Actor A: Is this your wallet you dropped? (extending her hand to B)
Actor B: Why are you holding that mouse?

The response changes the mimed object and therefore "re-creates" it. This status game says to the offering actor, "Your idea about a wallet is not as good as mine. You are not intelligent or creative. Follow my ideas only."

8. Some people mumble, talk too fast or mime badly.

This is fear and simply a lack of technical awareness. "If I'm not sure of what to do and how the audience (or partners) will react to me, I'm certainly not boldly going to throw my creations out to the public." Emotionally, that's obvious. But going back to respect for partners and "making them look good," none of that applies if they can't understand my contributions, either vocally or physically.

I don't like my young actors walking away from awkward demonstrations with only that as their achievement. Even if everyone knows the activity didn't work, I'll point out either C.R.O.W.E. elements or partner-centered principles and ask the actor to "do it again" focusing on one element to improve. All else still inadequate, the one improved item allows them to become a success rather than an "error." Emotional platforming and safety first, always.

9. Some offers aren't clear and the partner will freeze.

Beginning actors lack the critical skill to evaluate whether what popped into their heads will be clear, or (more advanced) if what they are making up on the spot is communicating to their partner. As a result, even if they had time to prepare, what they offer doesn't conjure the scene to the partner. So the beginning actor who must respond is stuck: "I'm willing to go out, but I have no idea what she just did out there." And instead of going out, the partner just stares, a smile of deathly embarrassment dawns, and the eyes shoot over to the coach as if to say, "What do I do?"

This is tough because everyone is somewhat of a victim here. The lead actor tried; the second actor wants to jump in but can't find "in." However, if it's handled well by the actors (stay good-natured), the audience will see the suffering and enjoy it because they know what's happening.

"But, still, what do I do?"

The second actor should jump out and do one of two things: accept some puny element that you think you might have understood and offer only on that, hoping that the partner's response will clarify something; or stay positive with whatever comes out of your mouth and with your body, and just go out into the corridor to be with the first actor. The error you can be sure not to commit is leaving the first actor on stage, alone, with the entire world knowing he's been abandoned. "I'm drowning and no one is jumping off the ship to save me."

The first actor can also read the terror and confusion in the second actor's face and continue the offer, seeking to clarify the inadequacy. You won't have to encourage this second effort because it's driven by the survival instinct. Will a drowning man shout twice for help if it'll produce a life preserver?

10. Some offers are vague and the partner boldly accepts differently than the offering actor intended.

Mistakes are our friends. Oddly, an awkward beginning such as this can end up producing some of the most exciting and novel work two actors might ever do. The key is to continue offering and accepting with each other on the edge of chaos. Stay good-natured and continue to ride the wave. As the coach, support the actors with your acknowledgement of the risk and ride they just took.

11. Some don't step into the corridor.

It's either fear or ego operating. Both actors are to meet in the middle, going halfway to meet in the scene. This is a metaphor for the percentage of responsibility each actor has in a two-person scene: fifty percent. Come halfway so you can be seen as a substantial player in the scene. Don't cross over to the second actor's face and crowd her out of the scene. Walk in halfway, and leave the other half for your intelligent and creative partner. Let her shine. But come in halfway to let her know that you are here for her. It's a privilege to work with talent. You are present for support, not ego.

#6 Scene Practice

If your training with young actors has followed something of the sequence suggested here, they are now ready to do scenes. "Corridors" showed them how to start scenes with an adequate C.R.O.W.E. and their skills with offering and accepting can keep the scenes going.

There are two things that are elementary but substantial for beginning work. The first is that fear will continue to show up in the scenes, not through blocking, but through the actors failing to accept the obvious action of their offers. What does that mean? Two actors will hit off on a scene that's, say, in a sandbox at the park. They are friends and eight years old. They have toys and things are going well. They will build a sand castle, maybe find something in the sand (perhaps a "key"?) and play for a moment. At some point soon, the actors get fearful that they've not established a "good" idea for a scene, and they will come up with something like this:

Actor A: Well, I'm bored.
Actor B: Yeah, me too. Let's go.
Etc.

What's the problem? All of the set-up information suddenly became worthless in the eyes of the actors and the audience feels cheated. Even if the scene went someplace else and engaged the audience's interest, we are left asking, "What was that sandbox scene for?" Can you imagine reading a book or viewing a movie and after ten minutes of exposition, the plot left everything established and went on to the real story? The critics would have a field day with that and so they should. Improv actors, like writers who take their time, should operate with unity and coherence. And they can.

So what was the obvious action in the sandbox scene that should have been developed? The sandbox and two friends are enough to get the two characters into a competition and change the relationship in some way. If they found a watch, certainly they can discuss it, where it possibly came from ("A man with a cane was just leaving before I showed up to play. Maybe it was his. I know him, I think. He lives in that junky old house one block away."), and that can reasonably set up the "search for the man" action. The boys might go (along with their

45

sandbox tools: buckets, shovels, etc.) to return the watch. (These goodwilled boys are certainly now our heroes!) The story unfolds.

Or, they start the competition to see who can build the coolest sandcastle, and as they dig deeply into the sand:

1. one falls into the hole
2. one gets grabbed by a hand under the sand
3. one finds a treasure map
4. one discovers a tunnel
5. one hears a voice under the surface.

Without belaboring the point, the sandbox is an idea, and all ideas have potential and actions they can invite. When actors get nervous about "what comes next," they have a tendency to toss the content.

Coach to develop the skill of finding the obvious action: suggest it to help them or ask the audience what an obvious action might be (the audience will have a lot of ideas because they are not on stage where nerves freeze imaginations). If you don't develop the skill in the actors, they won't get the skill. (That's profound!) Point? If the young actors leave the sandbox because they don't look for the obvious actions, they will go to another location, begin something and get nervous there. And they will continue to leave because they don't commit to an action.

Beginning actors create scenes that start, but they often go nowhere. They don't know how to begin, develop and then end a story line.

#7 The Form

Several of the games in this book require the teacher and student to have knowledge of the dramatic "Form." What is "The Form"?

Let's start off with what it is not. English teachers will often approach teaching narrative structure with the following terms: exposition, complication, conflict, rising action, crisis, climax and falling action. With those elements pretty strictly followed, or with some stylistic shifts here or there in that structure, most authors and playwrights stick closely to that template. At least it's a good starting point to note the basic similarities, and then variations on that form that distinguish creative writers.

46

When doing improv scenes or longer forms, the average improviser might find that remembering seven terms might be too much to hold in your head while you are also playing the scene itself and trying to work the requirements of the grammar game.

Way too much.

Here is what "The Form" is.

In improv, there's a let's-go-camping-and-pack-light version, or a *Reader's Digest* template that boils down the academic, seven-part template to four basic parts. And I think it'll surprise you how effective it is. I call it "The Form." The terms come from Keith Johnstone's book, *Impro*. (Read it if you are a teacher; it's a trip.)

The terms are pretty good in that they are almost self-explanatory:

Routine

Problem

Solution

New Routine

Here's the explanation. The hero opens the story with a life that is in its *Routine* phase. Now this might be a wonderful condition or pattern, but it's cyclical and what our hero is coping with. Now that *Routine* gets interrupted with a *Problem* of some sort. So, the hero has to go about finding a *Solution* to the *Problem*, preferably from the raw material in the *Routine* phase of the story. Once the *Problem* is solved, the hero is inevitably changed (dynamic character) by the experience, and he or she goes back to a pattern; however, because the hero is changed, the final pattern is somehow different and is therefore a *New Routine*.

Let's look at a simple example I'll make up based on something that happened to me today:

Routine: Tom got through the morning with the usual tasks of waking, showering, eating and getting off to school. He kissed his wife and then quietly said good-bye to his sleeping children, Nick and Melissa. He grabbed his briefcase, hopped in the truck and drove off to school.

Problem: As he was driving down the street toward the high school, he noticed a clicking and then a screeching sound coming from his engine or clutch. He pulled over to let the engine idle for a moment. Thinking that the sound might have been just a cold morning fluke, he pressed down on the clutch. Metal screamed, the truck lurched and the engine died.

Tom had no time to deal with the dead vehicle and no cell phone to call for help, so being only three blocks from the school, he grabbed his case and began to walk.

Solution: At lunch he called a tow truck to take the vehicle to the shop and then called home to get one of his kids to pick him up from school at the end of the day. When he called at lunch, a groggy voice answered.

"Can you pick me up after school and take me to the shop?"

"I have plans today," said the waking voice.

"Do you want to pay your own car insurance?" Tom asked calmly.

"I'll be there at four."

New Routine: The next morning Tom woke up, showered and ate, and kissed his wife good-bye. He then went quietly to the bedroom doors of his children's rooms, told them to get up, out of bed, into the shower, and eat.

He also mentioned that a list of chores for each of them was taped to the refrigerator door. Tom got in his truck and drove off, expecting a thoroughly wonderful day ahead of him.

#8 Typewriter (Belt and Stockley, pages 127-128)

This, like basic scene work, is an essential exercise for developing ensemble behaviors, basic scene skills and the elements of narrative. With a good introduction to these skills, many of the advanced games in the game section of this book and in *Grammar Wars: 179 games and improvs for learning language arts* will become a source of endless applications.

Explanation: One team has three to five actors. One member is the narrator, and the others are the physical actors (can use bodies and voices). The narrator sits to the side and mimes using a typewriter as she writes a story based on an idea from the audience. As she types, she speaks her thoughts, what she's writing. The narrator's words offer the characters and actions that the physical actors create on-stage for the audience. Simply, what the narrator creates, the actors enact.

Both jobs can offer for the narrative. Obviously, the narrator can offer as she speaks the story she is "writing." The physical actors can also offer by accepting the narration and embellishing those offers. (This accepting and offering shouldn't compete with the narrator, though.) The narrator might pick up by sound or sight something that the actors did that she could then build into the verbal narrative. It's not uncommon for the narrator to have no idea how to create the problem, so fortunately she can give opportunities to move the narrative to the physical actors.

One obvious way is to offer the physical actors some dialog tags:

Narrator: … so I looked to the salesman and said, …

Actor A: You didn't give me the correct change!

Actor B: Look kid, I gave you the correct change, and if you want to make a big deal out of it, go ahead! The manager's my brother.

Etc.

This way the actors (who are aware of the form and what elements need to be developed) can assist in moving the narrative to its middle and end.

Another way to solve the problem of the narrator at a loss for ideas comes from an idea Keith Johnstone shared in one workshop. Anytime a scene is in need of a problem, one of the actors can produce a sealed letter ("I've had it in my back pocket since … ") that either he reads or ("It's for you from … ") he asks the other actor to read. That mysterious letter engages the audience, certainly; the actor(s) obviously engage because they have to come up with the text of the letter, and the device gives some time for the narrator to work with the ideas the partners are developing. Sharing the task with intelligent, creative workers!

Other Exercises to Polish Basic Skills

Offer/Accept Drill

To conduct this activity as a training drill, have pairs sit separately so that they are not distracted by the noise from other pairs. Have one of them make an offer. The second actor is to accept the offer (try to avoid "yes" or "yes, and ... " because it sounds mechanical) and then must offer something additional into the imagery or details of the prior offer. The new offer is then accepted by the first actor who must add to the latest offer.

The challenge with this description is to clarify how this is different from simply "Yes, and ... " Beginning work with "Yes, and ... " often displays the accepting actor simply saying "yes" without building upon the offer. Every line (after the first one) in this exercise should accept *and offer*, not just accept.

Examples:

Adequate but not developed exchange:

Actor A: That man running from the bank! He's got a gun!

Actor B: Yes, I see it! *(This accepts but doesn't offer on to the creation.)*

Better exchange:

Actor A: That man running from the bank! He's got a gun!

Actor B: He's running towards us! *(Accepts without saying the mechanical "yes.")* Let's hide in this sporting goods store! *(Enhances the details/imagery of the shopping center, provides a specific response to the offer/problem, and will provide for some defensive choices — guns, baseball bats, etc. — for the solution phase of the story.)*

The skills demonstrated in the second example above, will produce a much richer C.R.O.W.E. context for the actors and the audience.

Sentence Completion (Levels of Continuity)

Same set-up as above. Two actors separate from all other pairs. One starts off with words (phrase, clause, partial phrase or clause, etc.) and stops. The partner immediately finishes with the words sufficient to make the sentence complete and sensible. The partner who just finished the first sentence starts a second, which the other partner is to finish.

Do this rapidly. Use this for developing spontaneity and listening skills. (Beginning actors are often guilty of not listening to each other.)

"Yes, and ..." Continuity

Set-up for "Yes, and ... " with this difference. The interrupt device is no longer the title words; rather, the interrupt must occur with a transitional word or phrase (coordinating conjunctions, such as **and, but,** or **or;** conjunctive adverbs, such as **rather, therefore, however,** etc.; transitional words and phrases, such as **additionally, equally, to a lesser degree,** etc.).

This takes time to get momentum in the play, because the new content has to have a more specific relationship to what was said just before the interruption. Speaking actors can be coached to speak more slowly here, giving partners the chance to "jump aboard" more easily.

English teachers: develop appropriate lists of coherence developing/transitional words and phrases and get your English students to practice this to improve logic and coherence in their essays and narratives.

Thoughts to All Reading Teachers

Reading as Rehearsal

Because I assume that you are a teacher (generalist, specialist, public or private education, or you teach acting in your community), I want to focus for a moment on one specific opportunity for integration with language arts. Yes, actors act. But good actors must be skillful readers. Improv actors need to be skillful writers, though they don't use pens, pencils and computer keyboards. For script work and improv work, the rehearsal and performance experiences are essentially the same: questions and answers. You will find that Keith Johnstone in *Impro,* and *Impro for Storytellers* uses the process of asking his actors about scenes and narration in training, and before and after performances.

And that is what teachers do in class. Basic reading skills teach students to look for and be able to support or defend two outcomes: facts and inferences.

Teach Reading Strategies by Teaching Students C.R.O.W.E.

Use C.R.O.W.E. to set up scenes and to interpret text. When training young actors to develop scenes and when coaching students for skillful reading of narrative and expository text, let the C.R.O.W.E. categories guide you to ask questions for facts and inferences. In both cases ask the reader/actors for evidence from the text to support their answers. With facts they can point to the exact word(s), and with inferences, they will have to point to two or more leading items and explain their thinking about what the text infers. If young actors don't think skillful reading is something actors and directors do as a key element of their careers, watch two different versions of one play (and if it's available, listen to the explanation for the interpretations), and you will find that both interpretations are grounded in facts and inferences from the text.

When preparing for and evaluating improvised scenes, ask the actors and audience for evidence of the C.R.O.W.E. elements. Require the answers to be backed up with references to facts and inferences from the performance. Ask the actors about choices they made about the location, the relationships, the emotions, and ask them if the decisions were made from facts or inferences they made in a split second just before or during the scenes. The improv actors in my English classes often produce the most sophisticated, defensible readings. But that comes from training and practice, practice, practice.

One of the first tricks to get novice actors going is the ability to make offers quickly that define or invite the specifics of the C.R.O.W.E. When a scene begins, it's nice for one of the actors to make a first verbal (or physical) offer that roundly sets up the scene. With practice it's easy to get going.

Example: Two actors stand on-stage. Actor A walks to actor B and mimes putting money in a sliding drawer, pushes the drawer closed, smiles and says, "Before you order, you might want to know that there's a ten percent discount on the Happy Meals for all senior citizens."

Let's just step through the C.R.O.W.E. elements, "reading" the offer. Make decisions (facts and inferences) from the offer made by actor A.

Character: I'm a senior citizen, probably my own gender.
Relationship: I'm a customer and my partner is a counter worker.
Objective: I want food to eat.
Where: *Things:* Counter, cash registers, illuminated sign above the clerk's head with several rows and columns of meal options with side orders and dessert options, "deals" for under a dollar, stainless steel kitchen counters and ovens, men's and women's rest rooms around some corner, plastic chairs and benches and tables, catsup in bags, soda machines, etc. *Relationship to the location:* Probably comfortable and familiar with the layout and products.
Emotion/condition: Hungry

Certainly there are other reasonable options. (Johnstone says there are many choices within the "circle" of options that the audience would expect from the elements in the offer.) Those listed above are a defensible set that works. Facts and inferences.

Weave performance activities, like the one described above, with narrative text. As the students practice, know the terms, understand the C.R.O.W.E. concept and develop their skills at asking questions, interpreting and supporting their choices, they can begin applying those skills to more advanced improv, acting with scripts, reading and writing.

Chapter 3
Assemblies and Workshops

Different teachers and schools are at varying stages of "readiness" when it comes to introducing something like Grammar Wars. Each has a "personality" that qualifies them for different first actions. Some teachers, for example, like to conduct playful exercises and activities, and so those instructors and students don't need basic tools to fuel up the play machine. In this classroom, students are offered opportunities to talk and offer ideas, and all those exchanges are safe: Students have been made to feel safe as they say and do things. Imagination is valued.

Some schools have a student culture that is either typified by immature students or by fear that drives an intense social grouping defensiveness. In the former, timidity and criticism exist to some degree and stay within the classroom; in the latter, aggressive put-downs and insults show up in exchanges outside the classroom, on campus and elsewhere. Most schools and classrooms stand somewhere in the middle.

When I anticipate working with a teacher, grade-level set of teachers or an entire school, I try to get a feel for the contact teachers on what they want to see happen and what their students are like. I try to keep in mind that with improv or Grammar Wars in an educational setting, both drive at "increasing student learning," or celebrating student learning. The goal (at least for me) is not simply entertainment.

Sample Scenarios

Teacher one is interested in the concept either for drama instruction or as an integrated tool that might help increase student enthusiasm or grab the interest of a small portion of a class population. This teacher wants modeling and demonstrations, and possibly training without students.

A process to get improv or Grammar Wars into this classroom or school might begin with an assembly by off-campus performers for one to three classes of students that would serve to demonstrate improv. Few to no students would be invited to play on-stage, though some might be used to time or support judges by honking horns. The assembly's goal would be to ignite enthusiasm and make the kids want more.

The next step (I like to do this) is to get into two or more classes, possibly at the same grade level (i.e., three fourth-grade classes) to conduct workshops with the students at that site. Prior to this, I check with the teacher to identify an English content standard that has been a part of their instruction prior to the visit. The workshop is then tailored to the language standards. I might do the workshop alone with the students and the teacher; I might also bring back the assembly actors to take advantage of the romantic admiration younger students have for older. We introduce the grade-level students to the basics of improv and their language content covered in the recent past.

This workshop gives some performance skills, shows the young students how to integrate the drama and English content, and importantly builds confidence and trusting relationships between the grade-level students and me or my student actors. Please note, however, that the combining of performance basics and English content is limited to a relatively narrow range of activities, some of which don't look like acting. For beginning students my first goal is to get them up in front and feeling successful and supported; my second is that they work, rework and rework the knowledge and skills that are the targets of the instruction. Finally, then, they are effective entertainers.

The next stage between classroom workshops and assemblies is class-to-class competitions. This would occur between classes that have had equal access to training and practice. Everybody in this event knows that it can be fun and nerve-wracking, that we support each other, and that there really are no winners and losers. Performance, but safe performance.

The final stage would be prepared assemblies for audiences (how big do you think?) who haven't necessarily been acquainted with Grammar Wars. This can be somewhat terrifying for novice performers, whether or not the audience is a group of strangers or "my friends." After some practice, the actors develop some confidence in the concept ("OK, I've seen that it can work well"), know which games will work well with inviting audience participation and how to end powerfully (in order to erase from memory the mediocre stuff that might have occurred in the middle of the performance). I require a lot of practice for my high school actors, and I require them to pass proficiencies on the content standards that will be a part of the assembly or workshop activities.

All this has been an effort to help you see that workshops and assemblies are different and meet different educational needs of each group involved. The first is a training; the second is a show resulting from training, skill, risk and learning.

So let me start by showing you one lesson draft for a workshop conducted in a classroom for fifth and sixth graders. Though there were two parts (narrative structure using beginning, middle and end; and paragraph structure) to this lesson, I will only review the template for the narrative section here so you can see one way to lay out the workshop or lesson.

Remembering that the goal is student demonstration of drama and English proficiencies, my goal will be to evaluate student learning of drama skills in the practice activities that they do in front of the class with a partner or two (nothing alone early on!). My goal for demonstration of learning in English will not be measured in the performance phase. Why? The school's job can be to have graduates speak perfect English, but that isn't how it's measured. Even newscasters and politicians do not speak revised and polished language on TV all the time (for some, not at all, ever). Extemporaneous speech invites forgiveness. However, when we write to get jobs, get into schools, write police reports, documents for international trade agreements, marriage vows, we have a higher standard for that discourse. Our students are mainly measured by their writing or reading. Schools and states measure learning in multiple-choice tests and student writing; therefore, that's the goal the workshops should shoot for. If you want to just go for extemporaneous verbal proficiency, fine, but know that an actor's ability to deliver on her feet in front of an audience doesn't necessarily transfer to demonstration on paper. Learning A doesn't necessarily equal learning B.

The Weave Model

To focus on the goal of written demonstration, I employ the Weave Model when designing a lesson plan. If you review the visual model below, you start at the top and work down alternating from side to side, or from written to performance to written to performance, etc., until you get the students to the written demonstration that is your target. Anywhere along the way, you can assess the ease and trust of the performance aspect of the lesson.

Different experiences I've had with teachers who've begun using Grammar Wars to teach English standards have told me that it is very important that your direct instruction and modeling of the content focus is essential to successful outcomes. The lesson starts there with clear explanations and examples of the English standards. At that point the "weave" takes over. For instance, if I were teaching parts of speech, focusing on nouns, I might do instruction and then ask students to write down on paper five nouns that are "things" around the room. Or to keep the weave activity on paper, I might hand out a paper with twenty words on it and ask them to circle the nouns only (*things* only, or maybe *things* and *places*). The activity is quick and it's a written form by which eventually, they will need to demonstrate learning.

Once that has informed me of any progress I need to see, I then *weave* to an activity that will prepare them for a truly performance-based activity. To make the transfer incremental, I might have an overhead prepared with twenty words, "five of which are thing nouns, and five of which are place nouns," I tell them. Then, to make this anonymous and safe, I put them in small groups (pairs, trios, table groups). When I flash the overhead with the twenty words, each group privately writes or just decides which five are things and which five are places. Privately, and safely. To be ultra-safe, I might go over the list of twenty in front of the class while the groups privately check their work with no public knowledge. From their faces and their papers I can tell if the knowledge and skills are sinking in.

If they seem to be getting it, I will continue the same game with one difference. I show a new overhead with a new set of twenty words. At their tables they are to write and categorize the five things and the five places. I then ask each group to stand and read their five (telling them there are five of each helps them check for correct and thorough results). Who will read aloud? Probably the most comfortable student? When we play again, another group member reads the choices aloud.

I might switch back to written format by asking them in their small groups (pairs) to take out their reading text, turn to page "X," and pick out all the thing and place nouns in a paragraph there. Share and discuss answers.

Back to performance practice, I ask for a small group to volunteer. They come to the front. I tell them I will flash ten words up on an overhead (why fewer than the earlier twenty?), and I will give them thirty seconds to find the three things and the three places. The clock makes the adrenaline kick in along with the attention of the viewing groups. After them, I ask for or pick other groups to play.

If things are clipping along energy-wise, we switch back to the written activities and I might ask the groups to make overheads of their own, imitating mine, that will be used on one of the other groups (this brings out their mischievous sides). Maybe I should have them read through some pages of their literature reader for interesting nouns and trick words to use on the overheads they're making. Which tactic would incite them to work with energy and enthusiasm?

Now we go back to the game using the overheads, with teams, a stopwatch and a scoreboard (if it feels safe). Showtime.

This game using the overheads, practiced by another class in the school, could be used if both classes got together to demonstrate, play and celebrate this skill together. I know this game and the practice would help my advanced placement students be able to check their writing for correct subject-verb agreement and sentence types. And believe me, my seniors need the practice!

On the following page is a blank graphic that might explain the Weave design.

Direct Instruction of Fact/Skill/Concept

Page	Stage
Activity #1— Understanding assessed — non-game	
	Activity #2 — Activity to reinforce the basic knowledge/skill
Activity #3 — Written demo with teams under time	
	Activity #4 — Performance application
Activity #5 — Written work for competition	
	Activity #6 — Competition using student-prepared materials
Activity #7 — Written demonstration	
	Activity #8 — Written or performed to respond to #7 formative assessment
Activity #8 — SAT9 Assessment	

See Appendix for a sample Weave for Misplaced Modifiers

Teacher two is interested and has some experience with activity-based methods, and is comfortable with having students create and perform. Possibly this teacher has some formal training in dance, drama, singing — but maybe just likes it personally and professionally.

If these students have been involved in performing any "up front" activities, we can assume less fear and initial resistance to doing things before their peers. So let's redesign the noun "weave" lesson explained earlier for teacher one.

Start with good direct instruction on nouns: clear explanation, good models.

The first activity following the instruction might be to get students into groups of five (I just picked that number) and have a writer for each group "secretly" (that word always adds some energy) write a list of ten nouns: the first five are things and the last five are places. I go around to check for lists done correctly. When all are done, I tell them to have a second writer in the group make "an *exact* copy of that list" so there are two of each list. They've talked and written nouns to reinforce the direct instruction, and there's a little mystery about the need for a second copy.

We weave over to using the student lists to play "What's in a Minute?" This is a charades game. The application of the game to our integrated purposes is that the list (the what) is designed to use aspects of our instructional focus — nouns. One group volunteers to go first. One of their members steps to the front, gets a list of ten that was written by another group and has one minute to convey as many of the ten to the other group partners as possible. So, to explain the odd title, to your teammates you try to communicate as many *what's in a minute* as possible. The actor can only use mime, gibberish, sound effects and melodies. He can't point to any real objects in the room. If sixty seconds isn't long enough, lengthen the time and the name of the game. Make your kids happy.

With this group I might keep score to use the competition element to make them want to practice, look up new, odd or challenging nouns, or to practice effective mime. If these kids also have this teacher for social studies or science, you might play the game with nouns that fit those categories. Drama, English and science all in one activity!

Back to a writing application in the weave model, I might do new direct instruction on the *persons* category of nouns. I might have them take out their readers or any textbook and sit in their teams (I'd probably reorganize their teams so no real team mentality arises that threatens winners and losers). With a stopwatch in hand and paper and pencil for each team member, we start. I say, "go," and each group has sixty seconds to find as many examples of nouns in the three categories (person, place or thing) from the text used.

At the end of the minute I ask each group to close their books, put all their answers onto one paper for the group (I want them talking about what they found, coming to consensus and rewriting the words — content review and repetition, over and over) and categorize the nouns into the three categories. When they are done, I have each group call out the total number they found and the number in each category so I can praise as many winner groups as possible. If any group doesn't shine somehow, I might note a unique noun they found that other groups didn't. Make everyone win.

Possibly I might weave back to picking up the abstract nouns (ideas) in the direct instruction and written work. You can imagine what activities might fit here.

Moving this group to a faster-paced demonstration of learning, I can imagine having the groups (reorganized again to keep the true team being the whole class) pick a paragraph from some source (no more than one hundred words). Possibly each student or group might write a paragraph of their own. Either way, the group should know what words in the paragraph are nouns (all three categories). So there exists the text and the "answers." Each group has its paragraph to use on another group. One group volunteers and goes to the front; each group has a horn. One member from the group that has volunteered their paragraph to be read, reads the paragraph slowly and clearly. The performing group's job is to honk every time they (or any one of them) hear any type of noun. If they skip a noun the team with the text notes the error. If they honk correctly at the noun, the teacher (or whomever) should note the correct response and give a point. Tally points and put on a scoreboard of some sort. To keep the non-competing teams involved, tell them that if a mistake is made that the reading team didn't catch, the observing team can point it out and get a bonus point for themselves. This way all students are engaged rather that just the obviously active teams.

Summary: This sequence is more aggressively performance-based than the activities for Teacher one described earlier. It will work to engage the more playful and risking students trained by Teacher two.

Teacher three is a drama teacher who teaches full-time drama or drama classes and some English/language arts classes. She likes acting and her students have experience. Some students are in both drama and English with this teacher. This teacher has students who want to do this stuff *now*.

The students here have done scenes as drama training or mainly as activities (does that make sense?). They are willing to talk on-stage and make up dialog. As a result, there is a whole battery of Grammar Wars and improv activities that open up to these students. Because you've already seen two weave models explained for you, I'll move more quickly through this workshop model spending more time discussing the performance activities than the written activities.

Beginning with a somewhat tame opener, I might suggest a modification of "Human Sentences" (*Grammar Wars*, game 121) in which we are only going to work the noun aspect of the spoken sentences. Two volunteers begin or I might demonstrate with one volunteer. At the front we get a scene idea from the audience, and the audience picks one category of nouns that we've studied in our English lessons. The audience chooses "place," and they've decided that the image of a house reinforces the "place" concept. To create that "house" image, they instruct us to create the location by positioning our arms above our heads, elbows out and fingers tips only touching together straight above our heads. (Does that look like the top of a capital "A" suggesting a roof?) So, every time in the scene we speak a place noun, the actor must make that shape. The use of the hand gesture can be "invisible" to the scene, or possibly for advanced actors it might have to be justified (the actors have to explain why they are doing the hand gesture within the context of the scene — for example, cheerleaders). The scene runs for sixty to ninety seconds. After the demonstration, the class is broken into pairs and practices. The class then forms a theatre layout with audience and performance area so that different pairs can demonstrate in front of the audience/class.

Assuming the students demonstrate at this point that they are comfortable with this activity and they have played it focusing on the other noun category types, we might then go to this next game,

"Traffic Jam" (*Grammar Wars II*, game 87). Again, I might demonstrate with a young actor or get two willing volunteers. The audience gives them one or more noun categories with which to work. Teammates of the two actors are given horns. If four noun types were assigned, then there are four horn honkers; each honker is assigned to listen for only one of the categories. The two actors do the scene in a limited time using as many justified nouns as possible, but points can only be earned if the usage is accompanied by a honking horn from a teammate. After the demonstration, groups are formed and practice separately. The theatre arrangement is set up again for group demonstrations.

Again, if this is a drama-friendly class, I'd like to let them really unleash their energy and animation. "Motown" (*Grammar Wars II*, game 88) is a great game to play at the end of a workshop with this class. A team of four or five stands in front with the speaker standing two steps downstage of the other team members. The audience offers one or more noun categories (say, places and persons) and a topic for the speech. Finally, they offer physical actions (and maybe sound effects?) appropriate for the two noun categories. (Hopefully, the audience will offer some wild actions that do reinforce the qualities of *place* and *person*.) The speech begins and the speaker might use a good number of noun examples so that the backup team really has to move.

In all three cases described above, at the end of a class session(s) with one or more groups, later that day or the next day, if possible, bring together the classes that have had the similar experience and have them work together in something of a mock performance/competition. Possibly, student actors from each class would feel most comfortable presenting with the classmates with whom they just worked. Sooner or later making teams with kids from the different classes reinforces the idea of "we're all here to support each other." If I come onto a campus with my high school actors trained in Grammar Wars, in the final presentation I will use them to encourage, perform for, or perform with the younger actors to make success and the desire to perform as strong a presence as possible.

It is possible, and likely, in situations where teacher and students are very new and feeling tentative, that at the end of the day I might have my traveling actors do what I call a "soft" competition. This is halfway between an assembly and a workshop demonstration, and in it my high school actors do performance games conducted earlier in classes so the audience knows them and new games that may or may not focus on the elements studied in class. The focus is still to build performance confidence in the younger actors, so the games selected will have "jobs" on the side in which we can use student volunteers, making them feel a part of the older students' work. Then jealousy will push all the other young students to volunteer themselves (now or back in classes later). Some games require timekeepers, scoreboard operators, horn honkers and whistle-blowers. These positions are safer for the cautious audience members, and we usually team them up with a high school actor to ensure their success and sense of team.

Assembly Structure

Any of the descriptions that follow are just models of things that have been done or that can be done. I've seen some assembly/ performance activities in professional improv performances, I've made some up myself, and students have come up with some wild ideas, all of which are excellent sources. And obviously, as students get enthusiastic about these activities, using their ideas goes a long way in making these performances and the classroom practice something they want to continue, and that will help them learn new content and reinforce learning over time.

The introduction of the emcee might begin the presentation (classroom or assembly), because it's a model students have seen and it sets the context/contract and expectation of performers, audience and applause. I tend to do the emcee work, but as soon as I can find a student who can demonstrate control of high energy, work with the audience (getting offers and volunteers) and monitor pace, I get the student to do that work.

Next is one of my favorite parts. The pre-arranged competing teams off in the wings are introduced to the audience. The emcee sets up the teams' arrivals and calls the names one at a time, after which the teams energetically enter then retreat to their sides of the performance area. The emcee calls up one team's captain, then asks the audience for a style which the team captain must use to introduce the members. The audience might be given examples of what "style" means, and it's good for the emcee to have prepared some workable examples (action film narration, romantic ballad lyric, play-by-play sports announcer, weather person, etc.). I've been quite surprised and pleased with what young students have come up with. The emcee can assist here by selecting an audience style offer with which the captains are actually familiar. Each team captain is given a different style. Whatever they are given, the team captains use that style to introduce their partners. It's critical, since this is the beginning of the performance, that the captains do this with enthusiasm and pace (despite how they feel). The team members also must accept the style and deliver their opening wave, smile, bow or action with energy. This opening image tells the audience that "it's show time and we're here to have a good time for and with you!"

Because Keith Johnstone got the idea of TheatreSports from viewing how people attended sporting events *en masse*, some improv shows begin in a traditional patriotic mode. So one way is to begin with the "National Anthem." After the energetic and playful introductions, the announcement of "Will you please rise for the 'National Anthem'" usually brings quizzical looks to most audience members. However, this is all a set-up for some odd, planned rendition of possibly some familiar TV show jingle with which all the audience members are most likely familiar: *Addam's Family* theme, *Gilligan's Island* theme, the *Flintstone's* introduction music, etc. The music is available on CDs through most music stores. I ask my actors once they start singing the lyrics to dance and march into and through the audience area as we sing with the music. This surprises the audience ("We thought the actors were going to stay on the stage!").

Let's look at some alternatives, especially if you have some talented or bold actors. The emcee might invite the audience to come up with some anthems of their own for one actor to sing. It might be effective if the emcee were to ask for the subject of a not-so-famous patriotic song topic, which one of the improv actors would then sing in a microphone as a solo. A national anthem or a well-known cartoon jingle that got rejected by the decision makers might be fun to hear. I also like the idea of two improv actors volunteering to sing into a microphone a "One-Voice" duet about our nation. ("One-Voice" involves two, or more, actors speaking at the exact same time trying to say the exact same words together.) Because these options are obviously made up on the spot, the audience sees actors who specialize in risk and who have little regard for correctness. We're here to play. At this point the audience is not sure what to expect but knows that anything goes.

The judges are introduced. They might be in robes to formalize their appearance and make them look out of place. They convey an arrogance and disregard for the masses, and they carry scorecards with 1, 2 and 3 printed on them. They judge for entertainment, technique and narrative in professional competitions. For the educational context, those criteria can be used if the judging students are well versed in reading for those criteria. For Grammar Wars, other criteria might be worthwhile, too.

The judges are to be the only "bad guys" in the event. The actors should remain good-natured and playful even if the judges' scores seem wrong. If the audience dislikes the scoring, and the actors don't complain, then the judges become the villains which makes the audience sympathize with and like the actors more. If, however, an actor with a wounded ego truly complains, the tone of the event turns ugly and self-serving, ruining the entire performance experience. The audience delights in seeing humble, playful characters that continually approach life with the spirit of a pleasant, resilient puppy. Let the judges be damned if anyone has to be hated.

I like to script assemblies for my teenage actors and for young, newly trained class volunteers so that I can ensure entertainment and success with the developing skills of both categories of performers. See the Appendix for a sample of an assembly script. Following each performance game is the English content aspect of the event. On the right side of the script are the judging criteria for the judges. If there are three judges but only two criteria, one judge is uninvolved. The model for a short assembly (forty-five minutes) involves only two teams.

A tournament of competing teams is another option. If you have developed a number of teams willing to compete from either one class or, say, two sixth-grade classes, then you can set up a tournament. All of the students and teachers involved should have agreed on the English standards that can or will be integrated into the performance activities, both non-scene exercises (i.e., timed recitation of alphabet or the eight parts of speech, or "What's in a Minute," etc.) and scene games ("Alphabet Scene," "Scene without a Letter," etc.). See the Appendix for sample tournament charts.

Micetro is a different approach to competition, and my instinct is to do it with your willing-to-lose, self-confident actors because it's more one-on-one than team — almost. The actors get scored individually in this format. Each actor's name is on a slip and in a jar from which the emcee or judges can draw. If the first game requires three actors, three names are chosen. The scene requirements are set and the actors go. The judges score the actors individually. The scoreboard with Micetro reminds me of those carnival games with water guns you use to squirt water into a clown's mouth. The more water goes in, the farther your horse (or rabbit or dog) travels along this horizontal raceway. The first horse across the finish line wins the race (and you walk away with a pink leopard).

The Micetro scoreboard looks like that. There's a horizontal slot (or set of hooks), and on the left are places to put each actor's name. When the game ends and scores are awarded, each performer's name moves to the right the number of points given. Names from the remaining actors are chosen for the next scene, and on and on.

Once every actor has performed, there is an elimination so that fewer actors remain for selection and the tension builds. After another round, more names are removed until only the day's thoroughbreds are competing, after which only one will win and take home the trophy (or carrot or expired coupon). So this form is more individual, yet the goodwilled nature continues and winners and losers are well supported.

A content-focused assembly in Grammar Wars centers all the exercises and sketches around specific language knowledge or skills (i.e., sentence structures and punctuation, or vocabulary [synonyms and euphemisms, paragraph issues, etc.]). See the Appendix for a list of games that support the essential skills for knowing active and passive voice. These fit into a lesson sequence for teaching the needed skills and then provide the games to play in a competition. The content-focused format only works well when the audience also knows (or pretty much) the content. Imagine an audience watching scenes requiring accurate use of semi-colons and colons and the related use of capitals with colons. They might feel out of it when violations occur. However, if they are "in the know," they will follow along and enjoy the educational snobbery of understanding the subtleties of the language! Parents try to appreciate a back-to-school night demonstration of advanced Grammar Wars, but often look a little lost or in awe of their fourteen-year-old who is nailing aspects of syntax and sophisticated punctuation issues.

To bring the rest of the audience into the event, use teachers from the classes in the audience or onstage to operate as judges and competitors: students will love to see their teachers suffer and mess up.

Finally, there are the free-for-all assemblies that are done for informed or indifferent audiences. These are often designed by the students themselves who choose to play their favorite games for personal reasons ("I'm good at it and can make people laugh," or "I can sing so I want them to hear me," etc.). There's nothing wrong with this type of performance, but because I am a teacher and students today spend a lot of their time being entertained already, I'd rather "kill two birds."

You might run this assembly with a theme, such as around WWF wrestling or Wild West. If your school has a theme project, this would be easy to fit in and support learning going on all over the school.

Other options might find the performance working from simple to difficult exercises, emcee-chosen games or team challenges where each team chooses the games to challenge the other team. If the audience knows various games, they can choose. How many options are there? Millions. Which formats are "right?" None. Experiment. Design a new format and email me.

Chapter 4
New Games

Games for *Grammar Wars II* - New Games Index

New Games

1. Shoot Out I (Claudia Reichle)

Teacher reads out a subject and the first team's player must come up with a predicate to complete the sentence. The teacher offers the next subject to the second team. Points are given for correct, complete sentences.

2. Shoot Out II

Two teams each develop lists of subjects (can be words or phrases: "Bob" or "the boy wearing the green hat"). Then the teams should switch lists and not look at them until it is their team's turn. Team A has one member read one item at a time from the list they received from team B, and different team members from Team A have to offer the predicates to complete each thought. Then Team B goes. Points are awarded for complete sentences.

3. Shoot Out III

Same as above but the predicate structures have to use an irregular (or regular) verb, possibly from a list of those verbs that the class has developed and put on the wall for all to see.

4. Shoot Out IV

Play the Shoot Out structure, but require some part of speech or grammatical structure in either half (subject or predicate section). For instance, you might require that in the predicate, there must be a prepositional phrase or an adjective, etc. The verbal offers can be done improvisationally or with prepared words and phrases as in I-III above.

5. Flash Card Conjugation Race I

Use various student-made flash cards with three items on each: a verb tense term, either "singular" or "plural," and either 1st person, 2nd person or 3rd person. One might look like this:

```
┌─────────────────────────┐
│        Future           │
│        Plural           │
│      3ʳᵈ Person          │
└─────────────────────────┘
```

Possibly the same terms are on both sides so when an actor holds it up to read it, the audience can read it, too. If playing against the clock, the actor holds ten to twenty cards, and working for the fastest speed, must create sentences that fit the terms on the card. Each competing player takes a turn. Whoever creates the most sentences while correctly using the terms on the cards in the shortest amount of time wins.

6. Flash Card Conjugation Race II

Same as above without the performance in front of the class. Instead have the competitors write the appropriate sentences for the cards given. This can be done either by a single player or a small team in competition against another team.

7. Flash Card Conjugation Scene

This can be done as an improv scene. Two actors on the same team have to use as many of the flash cards as they can, in order, within a ninety-second scene. Another team plays. The team that uses the most cards correctly wins.

8. Texas Toss (Dallas Thompson)

Players have to have been trained in active and passive voice. All stand in a circle, and one person throws a ball while saying a verb in its present participle form (i.e., running). The person to whom the ball was thrown has to state the past participle form of the same verb before or with the catch of the ball (i.e., run). The person with the ball then states another verb in its present participle form, and the process continues. No repeats of verbs.

9. Open Sesame — Timed Lists, Verbal

Parts of speech are listed on cards, one per. The written information appears on both sides of the cards so actor and audience can both see the items. In as short a time as possible, the competitor must create sentences that begin with the item assigned on each card, flipping the cards as they go until they have used each card. Each competing player takes a turn and the player with the shortest time wins.

10. Open Sesame — Timed Lists, Written

Same as above only done solo or in pairs in writing at desks. The fastest complete set of sentences wins.

11. Open Sesame — Scene

Same set-up as above but the actors in the scene each have a set of cards, which will control how they can begin each line of the scene that they improvise. The actors in each scene are on the same team and try to go through as many cards as possible in a limited time (ninety seconds, maybe). Then the second team plays. The team with the most lines with varied, assigned openers wins.

12. Super Heroes of the Grammar Wars

The audience assigns actor one a hero quality and assigns a world-level tragedy. Three other heroes come on to help solve the crisis. One endows two, two endows three, and three endows four: each with a grammar, part of speech, or punctuation fetish or obsession (i.e., commas-in-a-series spasm man — who uses many items in a series and who punctuates himself with some sort of spasm with each comma used).

13. Professor Know-It-All — Perfect Periods

Set up for the Professor team to answer questions from the audience one word at a time per team member. Each member of the team holds a balloon. Questions are answered and when one of the sentences ends, the member to speak the last word pops his balloon. That member can end no more sentences — only members with unpopped balloons may end sentences. A perfect play ends with all members ending a sentence and all balloons being popped.

14. Professor Know-It-All — Horns

Same as above only there is one horn that is held by the team member on the left. In this game players must speak in the order that they are standing. The first sentence must end with the member holding the horn. When they finish the last word in the sentence the horn holder honks the horn. The horn is then passed one person to the right. With the next sentence/answer the team has to get that sentence to end with the second player who will then honk. Then the horn is passed to the third member. The process repeats until the player on the far right holds the horn and the last answer/sentence ends there with the final horn honk.

15. Family Scene

Choose a word family (-oat = oat, float, boat, goat, etc.). Do a scene based on the word family using as many of the words in the family as possible. Each actor has to take a turn talking until they use one of the words from the word family. The scene ends after every actor has had a chance to talk.

16. Same Sound Scene

Choose a group of homophones (or homographs or homonyms) and do a scene based on the words in the group. Set a time limit for the scene (maybe ninety seconds).

17. Growing and Shrinking Sentences (Syllables)

Do a scene where the first line ends in a one-syllable word, the next ends with a two-syllable word and continue up to a four- or five-syllable word. Then the lines must climb down from a four- or five-syllable word to a one-syllable word to end the last line. This can also be done with the number of words used in the sentences of the scene.

18. Sound Scene

Two actors do a scene and each has to talk until they have used the required sound. Pick one of the following:
- The identified sound (i.e., "ē") at the end of the word
- Consonant blend
- Double consonant
- Digraphs (sh, ph, ch)
- Common roots (telephone, cacophony, stereophonic, etc.)

19. How Do You Get to the Met?

Two teams each send up one actor to compete. One is A and the other is B. The tasks are decided beforehand, so any needed props are available. A is the director and B must do the tasks, but B can operate within the ambiguity of language. The two are situated so that A cannot see B. Judges view to be sure B is operating within the parameters of language.

Example: The task is "put on a sport coat and button all the buttons." If A says, "Pick up the coat," B can pick it up with his mouth or knees, if nothing else is specified. The directions and actions continue until the speaker has given all the needed instructions. The actors then reverse roles and do the exercise with a different task. The judges or audience vote on which was the most effective in their use of language. Examples: brushing teeth, tying a shoe, putting on make-up, putting on a belt, combing your hair, using dental floss, etc.

20. NYC Cabbies

The teams listen to a paragraph as it is read out loud. The team members honk their horns when a sentence or conjunction doesn't fit within the context of the paragraph.

21. Punctuation Relay

Four teammates line up shoulder to shoulder facing the audience. The first one begins a sentence and one player from the other team calls out a punctuation mark which the speaker must obey (, . ; :) as they complete the sentence they began. Repeats for the second actor standing until all four have been given punctuation to obey. The process is timed. The second team has its chance. Fastest work with four sentences wins.

22. Road Map

A small paragraph with highlighted conjunctions and transitions (words or phrases) is projected and the team must come to consensus on which highlighted item(s) is incorrect.

Example: I felt my stomach gurgling and growling **so** I went to the kitchen cupboards to see what we had. On the lower shelf I saw crackers **but** peanut butter. **Because** I was starving, I put tons of peanut butter on a few crackers **and** ate them quickly. (The conjunction "but" doesn't fit; it would be better to replace it with "and.")

23. Conjunctivitis

After instruction on conjunctive adverbs, two players from competing teams do a scene. Each must offer a conjunctive adverb in a compound sentence before the next is allowed to speak. Sentences offered by each performer are counted; the actor with the closest ratio of 1:1 (sentences:conjunctive adverbs) wins.

24. Conjunctivitis II

Two actors do a scene speaking two-sentence lines (except for the first actor to speak in the scene who must only say a single sentence). Actor A speaks a sentence and stops, at which point actor B says a conjunctive adverb that is followed by a second complete thought. Actor B says another line, and actor A starts with another conjunctive adverb (can't do the same conjunctive adverb twice in a row).

Example:
- A: I like this little dog over by the swings …
- B: However, little dogs often yip and annoy the neighbors. I think parrots make better pets …
- A: Furthermore, they live in a cage and don't wander. I like that idea …
- B: Nonetheless, you're allergic to all bird species. (etc.)

25. Grand Central

A list of coordinating conjunctions is projected or offered (on cards) to each of two players. They are to do a scene and use all the assigned conjunctions, justified into lines in the scene. First to do it wins.

26. Comma Long with Me to Grand Central

Same as Grand Central but each actor must punctuate his compounds with a comma using a movement or horn where it belongs.

27. Kidnap

One player is given a topic on which to give a speech or tell some gossip. From the opposing team another player calls out punctuation, which the speaker has to use correctly. Similarly, the caller must call out punctuation where one might reasonably expect to see it (i.e., one wouldn't call out "semi-colon" after the speaker says only, "So Little Red Riding Hood told … ").

28. Conjunction Math

Players (one from each team) go to the front. The opposing team has created a list of conjunctions, either coordinating or subordinating (say ten to fifteen). The coordinating words make the items on both sides of the conjunction equal (=) in importance; the subordinating words make the clause to follow less important (< less than). As one team calls out each conjunction on their list, the performing actor from the opposing team must say either "equals" or "less than" after each conjunction called. The process repeats for an actor on the other team. The player that does the most correctly in the shortest time wins.

29. Conjunction Math II

Same as above except that the opposing team projects compound sentences on the board, and the performing actors must either identify the main clause(s) and subordinate clause(s), or place less than ("<") and more than (">") signs under the correct clauses.

30. Conjunction Narrative

This is a two-minute storytelling. A player from one team is to tell a story. A player from the other team has big cardboard cards with coordinating conjunctions on them which can be displayed only once each. The audience gives a title or content, and the story begins. Then the cardholder lifts a card for the narrator and audience to see (i.e., "and"), and the narrator must base the storytelling on that word (i.e., more heroes show up with the main character, or with "but" a problem(s) occurs or a surprise in the flow of the plot, etc.). Audience judges on the quality of the narrative.

31. Conjunction Typewriter

Same as above only the narrator has a team of players who act out the story as it is narrated (the actors may offer spoken dialog and obey the conjunction cards, too).

32. Birdwalk

Narrator either tells a story alone or with a team of actors. At any time the opposing team can call out "birdwalk," and the narrator (or actors) must deviate from the plot with irrelevancies. The opposing team can call out "story" and the original story must continue from where the birdwalk began.

33. Flashcard Narrative

The narrator (and an acting team) is given a set of flashcards with conjunctions on them (conjunctions are written on both sides of each card). Narrator cannot look at them until the storytelling has begun. When he begins he looks at the cards one at a time and must use the conjunctions in the storytelling as quickly as possible. The task is to use the conjunctions smoothly in the narration and tell a good, well-designed story (the Form). The second team gets a stack of similar cards in a different order and must do their own story. The audience (or judge) scores who won based on well-justified conjunctions and quality narrative.

34. Literary Corner, Honored Guest (Capitals in Titles)

A "famous" speaker is introduced by the emcee along with an honored guest, who sits in the "audience" (but the chair is on-stage). The special guest has a horn under his armpit as he faces the speaker. The speaker is a snob and speaks about literature and important books (using the titles). When a capital letter in a title comes up in the speech, the audience guest honks his horn for every capital (without knowing it). This is noticed by the speaker and eventually irritates him. The honker hears nothing. The speaker eventually says something about it. Rather than recognizing the speaker's complaint, the honker takes it as an opportunity to ask literary questions, to which the speaker initially responds, but with the continued honking, his irritation grows.

35. Cooking with Mutants (Professor Know-It-All Structure)

Four actors up in front, shoulder to shoulder facing the audience. A subject for a demonstration speech is given by the audience. The actors speak one sentence at a time starting on the left, going to the right, and looping back to the first actor (1, 2, 3, 4, 1, 2, 3, etc.). The task is that every actor's sentence must begin with an introductory phrase (gerund, participial, infinitive, series of prepositional phrases) that would require a comma before the independent clause. The introductory phrases should assist flow and coherence. Possibly the actors could make some sound for the required commas after the introductory phrase.

36. What's Missing? (Vonda Emmert)

Sentences are prepared beforehand having either subject and verb, only a subject, or only a predicate. Sentences are read to some team configuration. Each team has three cards: subject missing, predicate missing or complete thought (or independent clause, or dependent clause, etc.). First team with the correct guess wins. If an item is missing, an extra point is awarded for adding a part that completes the incomplete clause.

37. Die, Punctuation, Die (Chris Blakeman)

The players stand in a row, facing the audience. One person is the pointer, who sits on the ground in front of the other players. Each of the other players is given an ending punctuation mark. If more than three people are playing (with the exception of the pointer), alternate the punctuation (i.e., "!" "." "?" "!" etc.). The players are given a topic to talk about by the audience (the stranger, the better). Then the players begin to talk about the subject *only* when the pointer points at them. The people who are periods must use sentences that end *only* in periods. The same thing goes for the question marks and exclamation marks. The pointer can change people mid-sentence. The player who was talking *must stop* even if they are mid-word. The new player must finish the word and end the sentence with their own punctuation. If the player repeats, pauses too long, doesn't finish in their own punctuation or doesn't finish a word, then they must die. Their death must be original and dramatic. For example, they cannot die by being shot, drowned or stabbed, unless there is a unique twist to it, like being stabbed by a block of cheese. If their death is too common or unoriginal, you can demand a redo. The last remaining person wins!

38. Follow the Bouncing Ball

Four rows of five people stand facing each other (two sets of parallel lines). The first person in the first and the first in the third row are each given a ball. That person says a word (noun, pronoun, verb, future tense, adjective, etc.). That person then tosses the ball to the person in front of them, and that person has to say a word of the same word type before they catch the ball. Then that person says a new word from a new word type and first tosses it to the person next to the first person and it continues like that. The first team to get to the end wins. Penalties are as follows: If a person repeats a word type that was just used, the ball goes back to the beginning. If the ball is dropped, the person who dropped it has to throw it again using a new word type.

39. Punctuation Word-at-a-Time (J.D. Darnell)

Two people are on-stage. The two start Word-at-a-Time and when they reach a punctuation mark they must make it very clear that a particular punctuation mark is there. Assign each punctuation mark a noise or action and when the actor hits a spot where a mark should be, then they do the proper action or sound. If a person misses a punctuation mark, makes the wrong noise or action or misplaces a mark, then they are out of the game.

There can be teams to replace actors as they get out and the first team out of all their players loses, or it could just be a two-player game — you're out, you lose.

40. Balloon Toss

Two players (or more) have an inflated balloon. The balloon is bopped into the air, the emcee calls the category for the game (i.e., prepositions, forms of "to be," etc.) and the players must say an item from the category before they can hit the balloon back to the partner. If the balloon hits the ground, it's a fault and the game is over.

If the two players are on the same team, the number of correct answers is their total score. If the two players are on opposing teams, the one who let the balloon land loses.

Note: A light scarf or a tissue can also be used because they float. You can also use a sixteen-pound shot from the track team, but that changes the nature of the game.

41. Popping Periods

(Professor Know-It-All Structure) (Joe Bell, Carady Madden)

Two to four (or more) players stand facing the audience side by side. Each has an inflated balloon under one foot. They either just talk on an offered subject, or they answer questions from the audience. Regardless of whether the answers are one or more sentences, if a sentence ends with player #1 (or #2, #3 or #4), that player pops the balloon by stepping down hard.

Younger players: Someone then replaces the popped balloon with an inflated one and the exercise continues.

Older players: The goal is to create sentences one word at a time, yet have each sentence correctly end on each of the four players so that no two sentences end on one player. If the team needs to use colons or semi-colons to lengthen a sentence to try to make it end on, say #3, to pop the last balloon, then they might continue the sentence with another dependent or independent clause. They would have to justify that by saying aloud the punctuation needed as the words came out.

42. Edith Edit (or Eddy Edit)

Three players stand side by side and face the audience. The player in the middle has two horns, one under each armpit. The players on the side hold the center player's closest arm like the handle of a water pump. The two side players may either speak anything (a story, a review of last night's homework, a speech, etc.), but they must "honk" Edith whenever the required language element comes up in the speaking (i.e., if the target is capitals, then the speakers must "honk" Edith whenever a capital arises in their work).

43. Edith Edit Amputee

Choose one person to be Edith. Edith holds the horns next to her hipbones with her arms straight down. The other two people stand by her sides. The audience asks a question and the "non-Ediths" respond a word at a time. The catch is that for every capital letter and punctuation (ending or comma or quotation marks, etc.), the person that said the part of the sentence that requires it must honk the horn closest to them by pushing Edith's arms. If someone messes up, they lose the body part they were using to honk (i.e., right arm, forehead, left hand, etc.). Soon people will need to use knees, ears, wrists, chins, butts, etc. to honk Edith's horns. The harder and longer the responses, the better it is!

44. Sir Honks a Lot (Uses the Professor Know-It-All Structure)
(Jon Kenworthy, Cody Peters, Brian Kelley)

Three people are selected from one team. They are given horns. The emcee acts as the moderator. The three performers answer the questions from the audience one word at a time. The person who says a word that is believed to be the end of a sentence raises their horn and honks it. If the structure is a question, the first person and the person to the left raise their horns and honk them. For an exclamation point all three raise their horns and honk. The answers must consist of two sentences. Five questions will be asked. The rest of the teams, if any, do the same when it's their turn. The audience chooses the winner.

45. Helping Hand Action/State of Being Toss/ Active Passive Toss (Brian Kelley)

Choose an even number of people. Half of them become the bodies, and the other half become the hands as in the game "Helping Hands." The players form a circle. The audience chooses the type of verb to be used. The players (the "hand" actors stand behind the front actors with their hands pretending to be the front actors' hands) toss the ball to each other. The hands toss the ball, as the front actors conjugate the type of verb. This continues for two minutes. Then the other team plays the game.

The audience chooses the winner by speed of playing well, laughter, applause, etc.

46. Pot O' Gold
(Andrew Gonzalez, Carisa Ridgway, Leah Pezzi, Leann McCracken)

Three to four players are selected to play the game, and one host is picked to read the cards. The host is like a host on a game show. The game begins by having all the contestants stand at one end of a line (five feet long, maybe). The pot o' gold is placed on the opposite side of the line of players. The host begins the game by naming off book titles. The first person to buzz/ring/honk in with the correct answer (number of capital letters) gets to take one step forward (a step is determined by placing one foot in front of the other, heel to toe). There can be a time limit given, but there doesn't have to be one. Each person gets only one chance to attempt an answer. As the game progresses the first person to reach the pot o' gold wins whatever is in the pot.

47. Booktalk (Tim Nickless)

This game involves the rules of capitalization in titles. Before starting the game, make sure that students have a good initial knowledge of the rules of capitalization in titles. Have a few of the students go up in front of the class and sit down. They will be imitating a TV show that conducts book talks. Every line that they say must have a title of a book in it. The trick to the game is that every time they come to a capital letter in the title, they must make some sort of noise mixed with a gesture. These noises and gestures can either be made up on the spot or they can be predetermined by the player's classmates or teacher. There is no set length to how long the game must last.

Variations: One of my favorite variations is to put this game into a "Yes and ... " or a "Q and A" format. You can also ask the kids to explain the gestures that they use for the capitals.

Judging/scoring: There is no winner or loser in this game, therefore there is no judge and there are no points. You may alter the game in whatever way you like to turn it into a competitive game. This game is highly entertaining once students get it up to speed.

Other notes: Try to encourage whoever is playing this game to invent their own titles and stay away from highly used ones. Example: *One Fish Two Fish Red Fish Blue Fish.*

48. Vocabulary Bingo I

Blank Bingo cards are distributed (see sample in the Appendices). Each team member privately writes vocabulary words in the boxes on the blank Bingo card. One word per square. Each word can be used only once. The sample Bingo card has twenty-five squares; however, you can make Bingo cards with as many squares as you need. (To keep rows and columns equal, the cards should be 2x2, 3x3, 4x4, etc.)

Five speakers go to the front of the room. All the other players with Bingo cards fill in the five players' names, one above each of the five columns.

Each player one at a time will pronounce correctly one vocabulary word and define it correctly. When that is done, the player crosses out or places a penny over the word in the box *only if that player* used that word. Do not repeat any word from the vocabulary list more than ... (depends on number of words on the original vocabulary list). Rows or columns filled with repeating words from the list will not count.

49. Vocabulary Bingo II (Charades Type)

The same cards from Vocabulary Bingo I are collected by the emcee and redistributed. All players on all teams review the cards each received for correct spelling of the words. Team A will go first. One player from Team A gets a list of all the vocabulary words. Timer begins the game. The player must mime one of the chosen words and the team members guess the word. If they guess correctly, they look for that word on their Bingo cards and mark the square. The player goes to another randomly chosen word from the list. When one of the team members fills one complete row or column, they call "Bingo," and the clock stops so the emcee can check if the row or column was blacked out accurately. When one team member has completed a row or column and the time taken has been identified, that round is over and the second team goes. The second team's player cannot imitate/repeat any of the first player's mimed actions. Fastest time wins. (See sample Bingo card in the Appendices.)

50. Professor Know-It-All Paragraph Structure I

Set up for a standard Professor Know-It-All game: four to six actors are shoulder to shoulder facing the audience. The emcee gets a topic from the audience. The Professor actors will offer one sentence at a time (instead of one word at a time). Start on the left and go to the right. The first actor offers a topic sentence for the subject offered by the audience. The middle actors offer supporting materials appropriately fitting under the topic sentence. The last actor offers a concluding sentence. The teams earn a score from judges based on instruction and the appropriate grade-level achievement.

51. Professor Know-It-All Paragraph Structure II

This game is the same as above but demonstrates more versatility with paragraph structure options. The audience gives a topic for the Professor and the emcee or audience also gives a structure for the paragraph (i.e., chronological, spatial, topical, least-to-greatest, persuasive, arguments from facts cited, etc.).

52. Rewind (Essay Order)

Assuming instruction with the five-paragraph essay template, there are five actors side by side facing the audience. The actor on the audience's left does the thesis paragraph. The three in the middle (going from audience's left to right) do body paragraphs one, two, and three. The actor on the audience's right is to do the concluding paragraph. The emcee gets a topic from the audience. Going in reverse order, the actors are to "write" the paragraphs backwards, starting with the concluding paragraph and progressing backwards to the introductory paragraph.

53. Abbreviations

This is a scene with two or more actors where an actor has to continue speaking until they have used an abbreviation.

54. My Water Broke!

This is a two-person scene where each actor can only speak one sentence at a time. Each actor gets a point for every contraction used; the more in each sentence the higher the score.

55. Fragment Scene

Two actors play. Each can only speak in fragments. Horn honks and corrections required if there is an error.

56. Fragment Scene Elimination

Two teams play, but only one team member from each team is on-stage at a time. If one actor uses a complete sentence, they are replaced by a team member from the wings. The team with an actor left on-stage wins. The emcee can warn and eliminate an actor if the actor is playing safe and offering little to nothing.

57. Fragment Switch

Same as above only the emcee can do one of several things:
1. Call "switch" and the actors then have to speak only in complete sentences.

2. Assign one actor fragments and the other complete sentences. The emcee can call "switch" and the two have to switch the requirements. (Now the first has to speak in complete sentences, the second only in fragments.)

58. Completely Yours I

Two actors from one team do a scene. Actor A speaks the first portion of a thought, and B must finish it. B continues by starting a sentence and A must finish it. Back and forth. The number of correctly delivered complete sentences spoken by both (together) is the number of points earned.

59. Completely Yours II

Same as above but the two actors are from different teams. If either actor makes a complete sentence on his own, the opponent actor gets a point. Sixty- to ninety-second scene.

60. Snobs

This is totally a stupid game that is so simple. However, it's wonderful if the actors are willing to act arrogantly without being truly mean. Two actors take the stage. The emcee gets a part of speech or a grammatical structure (preposition, introductory phrase, articles, etc.). They are to do a scene where each line has to have the identified item, and the actor must say that one required item as if it were the height of intelligence, education, or rhetorical wit. The haughtier, the better. The more removed from significance, the better.

61. Effective Affectation (A Snob Game)

Two actors take the stage. They should be versed in the differences between the verb and noun definitions of *affect* and *effect*. They must do a scene (snobs) where each line must have one or more of either affect or effect correctly used and justified in the scene. The more correct uses, the better. Judges can evaluate on the spot, and if an actor makes an error, they must correct it on the spot immediately.

62. As If!!!

Two actors take the stage. Each has been versed in the difference between as (as, as if, as though) and like. Each actor must create dialog that uses one or the other (like, or one from the "as" group). Points can be given for correct uses, or negative points for errors. Use trained students as judges to reinforce the learning.

63. Name That Word I

This is a take-off on the show *Name That Tune*. One team leaves the room and the one to compete first stays. A category is given to the team (i.e., parts of speech, adjectives, weekly vocabulary list, etc.). The team player that has the words to convey is at the front with an overhead or a chalkboard. He writes down one letter and the team confers on what word from the category it might be. If they can't guess with certainty, another letter is posted. They guess or ask for another letter. When they guess, if they are correct, the number of letters counts negatively as a score. All words in the category are given and the total number of letters needed is tallied. The second team reenters and repeats the process, the words given in the same order. Lowest score wins.

64. Name That Word II

Similar to the one above only both teams compete at the same time. The emcee flips a coin to see which team goes first. A category is given. The emcee writes the first letter of the first word on the board. The first team gets a chance to guess first. If they guess correctly, they win a point. If they pass, the second team can guess or pass. Any time a team guesses and is wrong, they get a point taken away. Alternate, going through each word until all the words for the test have been used. The team with the highest score wins.

65. Close the Question

There are two lists of five sentences each. Each sentence is grade-level appropriate. Each sentence has one word that has been removed and replaced with one of the terms describing the eight parts of speech. The part of speech entered is *not* the part of speech that was removed.

Example: The boy decided to do his chores early **adjective** the morning.

The guessing team has fifteen seconds to decide the correct part of speech and choose an appropriate replacement word (i.e., "preposition," "in"). Ten points possible for a perfect score. The second team then competes with a second, comparable list.

66. Speed Dial

This game goes for thirty seconds each round. One (two or three, maybe) player(s) from the first team goes to the front. The emcee has a random list of the eight parts of speech with the parts repeated so that maybe the list is twenty items long. When the clock begins, the emcee calls the first part of speech and the contestant must offer a word that fits the called category. The emcee immediately calls the next part of speech. One or more judges are evaluating the correctness of the offers. The number of correct examples at the end of thirty seconds is the score earned.

67. Synonyms

A list of synonyms is projected on the wall so that the actors and the audience can see them (i.e., synonyms for "said": answered, begged, moaned, remarked, bragged, sighed, agreed, chattered, etc.). The team competing will play a typewriter story where one actor narrates a story and the physical-actor team members act out and speak dialog (when it's offered). The goal is to tell a story that follows the narrative form (routine, problem, solution, new routine) and justifies the use of all of the synonyms listed. The synonyms must be used with the correct, justified contexts and connotations. The task is to tell a quality narrative form, using all the required synonyms well in the shortest time. Judges evaluate each story for narrative and correct use of synonym meaning.

68. Parts of Speech Endowment

Two actors from separate teams do a scene together. First, one player leaves. The remaining player is given a part of speech to be obsessed with or allergic to. For example, every time the actor hears a coordinating conjunction (or just "and," or "but"), she gets a painful splinter in her body somewhere (has to be justified in the scene). The scene is played and the actor who doesn't know the assigned part of speech or word must continue to play the scene trying to identify the trigger word/category. Winning is based on the quickest time to identify the trigger word. The game can be played with both actors from the same team.

69. Group Edit I — Element Identification

This game brings students closer to real-world applications of editing skills as they will have to do in their own writing or in peer-editing groups in an English class. Use an overhead projector or some similar equipment.

Divide class into teams. Have prepared transparencies with single sentences or paragraphs already written. Following the initial direct instruction on one or more aspects of grammar, punctuation or style, show the overhead and ask the team(s) to identify a specific element. Fastest team wins.

70. Group Edit II — Success Identification

This requires the same general activity as above. The difference is that each team has been asked to prepare the transparencies. Each team has produced a readable text with successful grammar, punctuation or style traits that reflect the objectives of the classroom instruction. The emcee shows the overheads to another team who is asked to identify where the successful learning was demonstrated (i.e., parallel structure, punctuating compound/complex sentences, etc.).

71 Group Edit III — Error Identification and Correction

Same basic game as above. Here, however, teams have produced text that includes errors on skills that have been taught in class. Overheads from one team are used for the competitions of other teams. The overhead is shown, and the team is either told to identify errors (items covered from instruction) or to look for specific error types. The team with the fastest time at finding and correcting the errors correctly wins.

72. Sing-alicous (Pat Franco)

This assumes that students in the classroom are comfortable singing either alone or in groups. A familiar song is chosen. The singer(s) sings and another team member with a horn honks to show when there is a period. If the location of capital letters (or anything else) is important, you can have the honker or another team member do some audience-designed action to show the location of capitals.

73. Life on the Midway — Capitals (Stacy Reger)

This is a Professor Know-It-All structure. Set up four actors to be the Professor, answering questions from the audience one word at a time. Each time a word that is capitalized is spoken the player who says the word must change places in the line without interrupting the flow of the answer.

74. Life on the Midway — Commas (Stacy Reger)

This requires the same basic structure as above. However this time the focus is commas (items in a series, interjections, compounds, complex sentences, appositives, etc.). Each time a comma fits into the answer, the actor following the comma must spin in a circle (honk, bark, dance, etc.).

75. Proper Sneeze (Jessica Honea)

Two actors from the same team will improvise a two-minute scene idea from the audience. Their goal, besides doing the scene well, is to use as many proper nouns as possible. Whenever actor A uses a proper noun, actor B must justify a sneeze, and vice versa. The number of correct proper noun uses and sneeze combinations determines the points earned. The second team does their scene and the team with the most points wins.

76. Match Game (Professor Know-It-All Structure)

Set up for Professor Know-It-All (four people make up the Professor team). The emcee has laminated cards; on each should be a part of speech (noun, adverb, etc.). Each actor on-stage is given two of the cards and the audience can see the parts of speech. Questions are asked (or a story is requested), and the Professor answers. The actors' jobs are to see if each can offer a word in the sentence that also fits one of the two parts of speech they have been assigned. If so, the actor says the word and raises the appropriate sign. If they can't think of a word that fits the assigned parts of speech, they just say a word that fits the sentence and the answer continues.

77. What? Yes!!! (Joe Dawson)

This game is for younger actors. All sit in a circle and one holds a soft, light ball. The one with the ball looks at another person, asks any question using a strong questioning tone to emphasize the fact that it's a question, and gently throws the ball to that person. The person who catches the ball answers the question with an emphatic tone suggesting the emotional energy of the exclamation mark, or with a confident tone suggesting a statement with a period. All answers to all questions must be positive. No negative answers or neutral answers (I think so, maybe, etc.).

78. Sentence, Sentence, Sink (Chris Blakeman)

Sentence, Sentence, Sink sets up like Story, Story, Die (four or five actors face the audience). Here, however, each actor is given a sentence type (statement, question, command, exclamation, fragment). As the game is played, each actor when directed to speak must only use the assigned sentence types. Errors in sentence type or pausing or repeating at the cut-off will produce a "Sink!" from the director.

79. Inside/Outside

This sets up like Story, Story, Die. The exercise focuses on two different aspects of narration: advancing plot (series of actions related by cause and effect) and internal reflection (what is going on in the minds of the main characters).

The director gets a topic or title from the audience and off the story goes, told by each actor in turn as the director points. The initial focus is characters in locations and action. At the discretion of the director, she calls out "inside," and the speaking actor(s) must no longer advance the plot; rather, each is to reveal what the lead character(s) is thinking about objects, events, sensory signals, memories ... whatever. When the director chooses, she calls, "outside," and the story smoothly and immediately switches to plot advancement. At the director's call, the story goes inside and outside. The actors follow the narrative form to end the story well.

80. Scene without an Object

Two actors perform a scene. They can be from the same team or from opposing teams. Each spoken line (can contain one sentence or more) must end with a preposition. ("Where are you at?" "I'm standing on the floor you put me on.") Errors result from not creating a line with this mistake. Score appropriately.

81. Advancing Ladder (Verb Connotations)

Two actors do this as an advancing exercise, but the focus here is on the escalating connotations of the main verb in the sentence. Two actors square off. The emcee gets a mundane verb from the audience (i.e., "walk," "eat," etc.). One actor begins by saying a declarative sentence using the assigned verb, while miming it out. The actor stops and hands the response over to the second actor. The second actor is to come up with a verb that is denotatively the same as the one just used, but that has a higher energy (advanced) connotation to it. (Example: actor A said, "The young boy **walks** to the bus stop." The second actor to advance the verb says, "The mailman **jogged** house to house delivering mail." A third item for actor A to do to advance might be, "The dog **ran** after the elderly mailman." Judges or the audience should evaluate if the new verb advanced the energy. Possibly, one actor gives up because he can't think of a higher energy synonym to use.

82. Well, I Gotta ... (Noun, Adjective, and Adverb Connotations)

This requires the same as above except for two things. Instead of verbs, the competition focuses on either nouns, adjectives or adverbs. Secondly, it's conducted more as a verbal competitive conversation between two immature people.

Two actors go on-stage. The emcee asks for a noun, and the audience offers "man." The scene begins and one actor uses the core offer in its lowest connotative form.

A: My father is a **male** of the species.

B: Oh, yeah, my father is a **man**.

A: Big deal. My dad's a **jock**. My brother says so.

B: My mother says my dad's a **man's man**.

A: Remember the lady who almost drowned. My dad was the **hero**.

Note: This game can also be played with the offers descending down the ladder of significance (See *Most Low Status*, Belt and Stockley, page 156).

Example: (word offered: jobless)

A: My big brother's **unemployed**.

B: Big deal, my whole family is **economically indifferent**.

A: My uncle's **inertia-prone**.

Etc.

83. Simply Compound

Two actors do a scene. Actors should try to speak only one sentence for each line before alternating. Each spoken line should only be a simple sentence; however, the actors should either have a compound subject or compound verb in each spoken line. No compound or complex sentences.

84. Syntax Twins

This might be used as an intermediate to advanced exercise and performance game. Two actors from the same team go to the front. The emcee gets a story title and a sentence structure type (simple, compound, complex, compound-complex). One word at a time the duo is to tell the narrative following the *form*, while every sentence they speak (remember! word at a time) must be the sentence structure type they have been assigned. Each actor has a horn so that they can establish an end mark (period, question mark, etc.) with the horn honk. The game is timed (say a two-minute limit to finish the story).

85. Don't Let It Dangle

Teams prepare ten sentences on a list. On each list is a note about what the errant modifier is or a note that the sentence is correct as is. Each sentence may or may not have a dangling or misplaced modifier. In competition each team will use the list(s) developed by the other team.

Introductory form: Sentence lists are prepared for the overhead projector so teams can see the sentences and talk about them. Sixty to ninety seconds for each list (or more).

Advanced form: Sentence lists are read aloud without being projected so team members have to listen. Sixty to ninety seconds for each list (or more).

86. Spot Change

Two actors from a team go up front. The emcee has prepared sentences, or the other team has prepared sentences (list of ten). The emcee calls a part of speech or structure (prepositional phrase, dependent clause, etc.) and reads the first sentence. The team members are to identify the part of speech or structure called for and say the sentence aloud having changed the item called for.

Example:

Emcee: "Verb." "I have a dog in my coat pocket."

Team: (confers) "Have. I hid a dog in my coat pocket."

87. Traffic Jam

Two actors do a scene set up by the audience. They are given a part of speech (i.e., nouns, active verbs, irregular verbs, syntax structure, etc.) to use frequently in their spoken lines. A team member or two are given horns to honk every time one of the actors uses the required part of speech. Each correct usage paired with a horn honk earns a point. In a sixty- to ninety-second scene, the actors try to develop the scene and use the required element.

88. Motown

One actor is in front and four actors are upstage in a row; all face the audience. The downstage actor will give a sixty-second speech, the topic given from the audience. The audience identifies one or more noun categories and designates physical actions for each. When the speaker uses a noun, the back-up team must all do the movement together, energetically.

89. One-Voice Horns

Two actors stand facing each other. Together they hold the bulb of one horn so they can (or have to) honk it together to represent any endworks (periods, qustion marks, etc.). The audience offers a part of speech or structure (prepositional phrase, appositive, etc.) which the two actors are to try to use as many times as possible. The challenge is that the pair should speak each word simultaneously. The trick is to listen prophetically, watch your partner's mouth, and give and take with an equal balance.

90. Tag Team

Two teammates go to the front. Each, hopefully, has the eight parts of speech memorized. The emcee calls one of their names. That actor is to say the eight parts of speech one at a time, and after each one is said the partner is to give one (or two or three, maybe) example(s) of that category. When all eight have been called and an example given, the length of time used is called. Fastest time between teams wins.

91. Graphic Performances

Two teammates go up to do a scene. The emcee gives a physical or vocal action that the speaking actors must perform whenever a capital letter shows up in the spoken lines (i.e., capitals at the beginning of a sentence, proper names, etc.). The emcee also gives a sound effect for the periods at the end of each spoken sentence, which the actors must perform. (Good game for serious scenes.)

92. Flash Cards I

One team has cards identifying four sentence types (statement, question, command, exclamation). The emcee reads a sentence aloud (shows it on overhead), and the team confers on the type and holds up the correct card for a point. This continues for sixty seconds. The team with the most correct decisions wins.

93. Flash Cards II

One team has cards identifying four sentence structures (simple, compound, complex, compound/complex). The emcee reads a sentence aloud (shows it on overhead), and the team confers on the type and holds up the correct card for a point. This continues for sixty seconds. The team with the most correct decisions wins.

94. Flash Cards III

Set up like Professor Know-It-All with two or more players from the same team. The emcee calls out a sentence structure (statement, question, command, exclamation), and the actor on the left gives a correct example of that type. Another sentence type is called to the second actor who is to give a correct example of that type. This continues to actors three and four and loops back to actor one until the time limit is up. The number of correct answers is the number of points earned.

95. Flash Cards IV

Set up like Professor Know-It-All with two or more players from the same team. The emcee calls out a sentence structure (statement, question, command, exclamation) and the actors must give an example, one word at a time, of that type. Another sentence type is called and the process continues until the time limit is up. The number of correct answers is the number of points earned.

96. Drop Out III (Vice Versa)

Two players from opposing teams go onto the stage and are given a scene to play. The task is for the conversation to occur at a natural pace while the characters must reverse their use of subjects and objects (the cases must be reversed).

> A: Me see that you're ready to see the doctor now, Mr. Everets.

B: Him is late for the appointment again. Me is mad at he.

A: Me understands. The other patients, them has been angry about the doctor's schedule all week.

B: (etc.)

97. What's in a Minute II

(Same set up as "What's in a Minute.") "What's in a Minute II" must be played after "What's in a Minute," using the same list of terms (i.e., parts of speech). The list's order is mixed, but the performer cannot repeat any of the actions that worked before in "What's in a Minute." Between playing the two games, give the performer (and maybe another teammate to work with him) a few minutes to review the terms/concepts to develop another mime approach for this second round. The idea is to hit the term/concept from several different descriptions, forcing the team to understand the concept, not to memorize the mime bit.

98. Grab and Group

Project a list of words on the wall. One of the competing teams plays by sending up a single player, or they work as a group and confer on their answers. The emcee offers a category of which some of the projected words are a part (i.e., the emcee says, "nouns" and the projected list has some nouns in it). The player(s) responds with their answer as fast as they can, after which the emcee offers a second category beginning the second task. There is a time limit.

99. Count on Me

Two actors from the same team go up front and are given the requirements for a scene. One actor is given a part of speech (i.e., nouns) and the second is given another to use (i.e., verbs). They are to do a scene for sixty to ninety seconds. Each gets a point when her required part of speech appears in her lines. Judges count to determine the number scored.

100. Con-ju-gate Any Faster Than That?

Player goes to the front. The emcee gives a verb tense (or tenses). Possibly a chart is projected on the wall that shows the singular and plural pronouns in some order. As the timer begins, the emcee calls one verb at a time to the player, who must conjugate the verb correctly in the required tense(s). When the first task is done, a second verb is called out, and the game continues. Points are awarded for the number of correctly conjugated examples in the time limit.

101. Quartet Flash

Four teammates go to the front. Two are actors and prepare for the scene. The remaining two hold flash cards, one saying "singular" and one "plural." Each flasher is assigned to one actor. If the actor assigned to flasher A speaks a sentence using a singular noun ("I" or "it"), the flasher shows the "singular" card. If the speaker uses a plural subject ("we" or "Sally and Miguel"), the flasher shows the "plural" card. The scene has a time limit. Judges score for correct labeling.

102. Doorbell Punctuation I

Four members of a team go on-stage. The audience suggests an idea for the scene. There are three characters and the fourth member does sound effects (the doorbell "ding-dong"). The emcee chooses a punctuation mark that will trigger the sound effect. For example, the comma is chosen. Any time an actor says a sentence with a comma in it, the off-stage actor makes a "ding-dong" sound into an off-stage microphone. That event must be built into the scene by incorporating an entrance. Actors can learn to control the level of chaos of entrances and exits by their syntax.

103. Doorbell Punctuation II

Same as above only two or more punctuation marks are targeted for sound effects. To achieve this, a number of sound effects actors are off-stage to listen for and give the sounds. For example, three punctuation marks are chosen: period, comma and quotation mark. There are three sound effects makers off-stage. When sound person one hears a period, she makes the sound of a baby crying; when sound person two hears a comma, she makes a doorbell sound; and when sound person three hears a quotation mark, she makes the sound of a phone ringing. All the sound effects must be built into the scene.

104. Scavenger Hunt II

Separate sentences, or a paragraph, are projected or handed out to the players on one team or both teams if they are doing the task at the same time. Each player is told to find the items (or the number of items) in the text. For example, each might be asked to count the pronouns, adjectives and conjunctions in a paragraph and list the three separate numbers on lines at the bottom of a piece of paper. The papers from each team are collected and the number of correct answers is tallied. The team with the most correct answers wins. (See sample in Appendices.)

105. Pardon My Irregularity (Claudia Reichle)

From a secretly prepared list of irregular verbs, the emcee will offer verbs in the infinitive form to the players. Two actors from one team go to the front. They will have twenty seconds. The emcee calls out from the list the infinitive form of an irregular verb. The two players must give two sentences; the first must use the present tense of the verb, and the second the past tense form of the verb. The emcee gives another infinitive verb and the competition continues. The score is the number of correct, complete responses in twenty seconds.

106. Bran Muffin Scene

Set up a word wall on one side of the room with regular verbs listed. Get one team of four or six on-stage and put half on each side. Set up the scene with ideas from the audience. Give horns to judges to honk if any irregular verb is used in the scene. The emcee can call "warning!" for pauses or safe behavior (doing anything that limits talking because when they talk, they run the risk of getting honked). The two actors begin the scene. If either one uses an irregular verb (in the main clause), one of the judges honks, that player is replaced, and the replacement actor must alter the erring line to get rid of the irregular verb. In ninety seconds, how many acceptable lines were spoken? That's the team's score for that round. Rotate actors on-stage with actors off-stage.

107. Bran Muffin-less Scene

This is basically the same as "Bran Muffin Scene" only with irregular verbs.

108. Backwoods Poetry

A list of irregular verbs is placed on a word wall. Two actors approach the front to "recite" a poem derived from a title offered by the audience. The trick is that the verbs in the main clauses (or at least one verb in each spoken sentence) must be an irregular verb pronounced as if it were a regular verb (i.e., "wrote" would be pronounced as "writed" and "was" becomes "beed").

109. Alphabet Scene — Verbs

Same game as the normal "Alphabet Scene," but the alphabet sequence is found in the verbs, not in the first letter of the first word of each line.

110. Yes, and ... Conjunction (or Transition)

This is a derivation of the standard "Yes, and ... " game. On a word wall, put examples of conjunctions (and/or transitional phrases). Now play "Yes, and ... " with conjunctions (or transitional phrases) in place of the normal interrupter, "Yes, and ... ".

111. Paraphrase

Two actors from the same team go up to the front. One is giving a speech or selling a product. The partner paraphrases what is said in one of several possible ways. The spoken lines alternate one at a time.

Example 1: Synonym
The speaker is talking about his childhood memories of the good ol' days. The paraphraser is to provide a synonymous paraphrase.
Speaker: In Wisconsin back in 1945, life was tough.
Paraphrase: In the upper Midwestern state when I was a

child, everyone worked even from a young age
to help support the family.

Etc.

Example 2: Antonym

The speaker is talking about his childhood memories of the good ol' days. The paraphraser is to provide a paraphrase that reverses every fact.

Speaker: In Wisconsin back in 1945, life was tough.
Paraphrase: In Texas several decades in the future, death was easy to obtain.

Etc.

Example 3: Romanticized

The speaker is talking about his childhood memories of the good ol' days. The paraphraser is to provide a paraphrase that romanticizes every fact.

Speaker: In Wisconsin back in 1945, life was tough.
Paraphrase: In my favorite state, the land of cheese, the year that we were finally safe from the ravages of the war, life was a blessing to everyone as we all worked sixteen-hour days to make our communities vibrant healthy places to live.

Etc.

112. Endmark Tones

Two actors get up to do a scene. The performance bit is that they are to jointly respond to the end of each sentence spoken with the tone of the endmark. Since a period represents a statement, the tone by both actor will be confident. When either actor's line is a question, the actors strongly react with confusion. If the sentence is an exclamation, then both react with shock, surprise or amazement. This might be a ninety-second scene.

113. He Said, She Said with Punctuate Your Neighbor

(*Grammar Wars,* page 53)

"He Said, She Said" is a two-person scene where after each spoken line, the other actor offers a narrative tag giving the speaking actor an action to do in the scene.

Example:

A: I'd like you to fill out this first time visitor form, if you would.

B: She said while scratching her right arm compulsively. Do you have a pen I could use?

A: He asked, eyeing her brassy red hair. Right over by the counter.

B: (Etc.)

"Punctuate Your Neighbor" plays with two actors doing a scene. During the exchange when actor A finishes speaking a sentence with a period (or using a comma, etc.), the partner performs the audience-given sound/action for the punctuation.

To play this combination, act as though you are playing "Punctuate Your Neighbor." However, when the assigned punctuation (or part of speech) shows up in actor A's line, actor B offers the action tag as in "He Said, She Said."

Example: (The audience has said to work with commas in compound sentences.)

A: Get your license and registration out of the glove box, (comma precedes the coordinating conjunction) ...

B: He said, resting his left hand on the revolver's handle,

A: ... and hand it to me.

B: My wife's pregnant, (comma) ...

A: The driver said as he rubbed the woman's round belly,

B: ... and her water broke twenty minutes ago.

A: (Etc.)

114. Periodic Mood Swings

Two actors take the stage to do a scene. The three moods of sentences are projected on the wall in some order from top to bottom (i.e., imperative, indicative, subjunctive). The scene begins, and the first actor must speak a sentence that is in the imperative. Below that is "indicative," so the second actor must respond in the indicative mood. The third sentence must be in the subjunctive, and then the next sentence goes back to the top and must be imperative. The scene goes for sixty to ninety seconds.

115. Story, Story, Out (Paragraph Styles)
(See *Grammar Wars*, page 78)

Four actors are shoulder to shoulder facing the audience. A director sits between the actors and the audience and points to one actor at a time. When pointed to, the actor(s) speaks the events of the story (or the product advertisement pitch, the weather report, etc.). When the director switches to another actor, the previous halts and the new actor speaks picking up from the cut-off.

With "Paragraph Styles," prior to beginning, each actor is given a paragraph style or purpose with which he is to speak when it is his turn. If they are all working with narrative paragraphs, each has a different tone or style. If the paragraph type is expository, one might explain a process, another just an idea, the next an extended definition of a word or concept, or the fourth, facts or appeals to persuade. If descriptive paragraphs are the focus, each actor might be assigned to develop one of the following to do: describe a person, a place or a thing.

116. Timed Lists

This is a generic game structure where either two teams or single players from two teams compete by offering as many of the items in question (i.e., action verbs, forms of "to be," etc.) as possible within a limited time, or within a shorter amount of time than the other team's player.

117. To Be or Not to Be

Two actors take the stage and are given an idea for a scene. Neither actor can use any form of the verb "to be." The emcee or a judge honks a horn if the verb shows up.

Option: Set up the scene as indicated above, but require all sentences to *have* a form of "to be."

118. To Be

This is a timed list game where single players or whole teams are to list as many conjugated forms of "to be" as possible in the shortest amount of time.

119. Drop Out

Two players from opposing teams go to the front where the emcee gives them a scene to perform. In the sixty- to ninety-second scene the actors must speak all sentences with incorrect subject-verb agreement. Correct agreement is counted as an error by the judges.

120. Drop Out II

Two actors take the stage. The emcee gives an idea for a scene. The emcee identifies a grammatical rule that all players know (subject-verb agreement, consistent tense, complete thoughts, use of past participle [not the past-tense form] with helping verb "to have," etc.). The actors must do a scene where each spoken line, that can be more than one sentence, has to have the error version of the rule identified above.

121. Tense Scene

An agreed-upon number of actors from one team goes to the front. Each is assigned a different verb tense, or all are given one tense. The emcee gets an offer from the audience for the scene. The actors do the scene with a time limit, and each must use only their assigned tense.

122. Back to the Past

This is a two-person scene where every line spoken has to have the first verb in the present and the second verb in the past. Then the next actor may speak a line.

For example:

    A: I like that dog of yours. Mine just died recently.
    B: I'm sorry to hear that. I was thinking you had been sad lately.
    A: (Etc.)

123. Counterpoint Participles

Each team prepares a list of twenty participles, possibly combinations of present and past. The list is given to one member of a pair of actors from the opposing team. Use a clock to time. The performer with the list reads the participles to the teammate who must give the other participle form of the word read (i.e., A reads "running," followed by B saying the past participle form, "run," etc.).

124. Voices

Two actors take the stage and are given an idea for a scene. The scene proceeds. The emcee has assigned some combination of required voices from the two actors: One must speak only with passive voice while the other must speak only in active voice. The emcee can call "switch."

125. AP Reduction Relay

A team of five (can be any number) writes out a list of five sentences in the passive voice that are numbered and prepared for overhead transparencies. The opposing team, each of whom is numbered one through five, is shown the overhead and is given ninety seconds to write out active voice revisions for the assigned passive sentences. When the clock stops, the correct revisions are tallied. For every correct revision, the team gets a point. The process repeats for the second team. At the end of play, the team with the most points wins.

126. Human Paragraphs

Send five actors to the front, shoulder to shoulder facing the audience. From left to right each actor has a job to accomplish with just one sentence. The team is given a subject, and they must create a verbal paragraph that develops that subject. The first actor (on the left) delivers the topic sentence. The next actor to the right delivers the first supporting content sentence fitting that topic sentence. The third and fourth actors deliver the next supporting content sentences, and the fifth actor delivers a concluding sentence that provides closure and reflects the content and perspective of the previous sentences.

A second team plays and the judges score on unity, transitions, coherence — whatever the elements of the instruction included.

127. Opener-Sesame

A set of cards is given to each of the two performing actors. Each set has eight cards, each with a part of speech printed on both sides. The order of each set is random.

The two actors are to conduct a scene built on an idea from the audience. Each line spoken by each actor must begin with the part of speech listed on the actor's top card (which is held so the audience can see it, too). After a card is used, it is placed at the back of the set of cards, so the cards rotate around and around as each actor speaks and the scene continues. Set a time limit, within which the scene must come to a conclusion.

Judges score on natural speech and correct use of parts of speech.

128. Four-Sentence Scene II

Two actors go on-stage. Each is given a list of sentence types, and each of the two lists has the types in different orders. (Actor one has "simple, compound, compound-complex, complex" while actor two has "compound-complex, complex, simple, compound.") They do a scene from an audience suggestion, and the spoken lines from each actor must follow the syntax types, in order, from the assigned list.

Determine a time limit for the scene. Judges score on natural speech and using the correct types of sentences.

129. Tone Challenge I

One actor from each team goes to the front. They take turns giving impromptu speeches. Each is given twenty points. A list of words is projected so the speaker and the audience can see it. The list is made up of words (or phrases, metaphors, etc.) that suggest a clear tone (power, joy, depression, etc.). The speaker is either given the implied tone in which to speak or is allowed to choose a tone that they feel fits the projected list. The topic is offered to the speaker or they can make one up. The actor must use all of the words and stay within the suggested tone or they lose points. The second actor gets a new set of words and a new tone. The actor that loses the least amount of points wins.

130. Tone Challenge II

This is essentially the same as "Tone Challenge I"; however, the emcee or audience requires the speakers to deliver their speeches in performed tones that are the opposite of the projected words (phrases) on the list. For example, the words might fit a child's birthday party, but the assigned tone is depression or manic fury.

131. News Report Mutant I

Three actors from the same team sit in front as news anchors. Each event reported consists of three sentences. The emcee or audience offers the number of reports (i.e., three) in the news segment before a commercial break. The actor on the audience's left makes the first sentence of the report, which includes a common noun ("a man was arrested today for trying to kidnap a goat"). The middle actor offers the second sentence of the report by defining the common noun with a more specific proper noun (i.e., "Robert Beardly refused to answer all questions while being detained at the county jail"). The actor on the audience's right offers the third and final sentence replacing the common noun with an appropriate relative pronoun (i.e., "the alleged kidnapper, who goes by the name Hoover, will be arraigned at week's end").

Judges score on smoothness of the three-sentence delivery and the correct shift and use of the nouns and pronouns.

132. News Report Mutant II

The same setup is used as in "News Report Mutant I." Between the performers and the audience are three short posts with red light bulbs on top, each electrically wired to a switch controlled by the emcee. With the switch, one light is on at a time. This light works as the "on" light on the studio cameras. When one light is on, the mutant reporter(s) must look at that camera. When it switches, all three of the news anchors must look to the new "on" camera.

133. One Voice: Timed Sentences

Two (or more) actors face each other, or make a horseshoe if the audience needs to see their faces. To perform a "one voice" exercise, the actors look at each other and try to all say the same words at the exact same time to form sentences and stories (whatever the goal is). The emcee has a stopwatch and gives the team a limited time (sixty seconds) to say in "one voice" as many sentences (single clauses, sentences with prepositional phrases) as possible. The second team then competes. The team with the most acceptable sentences wins.

134. Sign Language (Parts of Speech) (Joe Bell)

Two teams prepare by privately deciding on gestures that represent the traits of each part of speech (i.e., many verbs are action words, so the team's gesture might be running in place; for conjunctions they might have an actor make a plus sign with two hands).

Two members from team A go to the front and tell a story one word at a time. Two members from team B are assigned two parts of speech to listen for. When that part of speech occurs in the story being told, the two actors from team B must each do the sign for the parts of speech they are detecting. Correct responses from the signing team earn them points; missed examples cause the team to lose points. Then team A and team B must switch roles so that the B team members are telling the story and the A team members are signing the parts of speech.

Chapter 5
Maximizing Student Involvement

Take No Prisoners!

If you have thirty students in your class, it is a waste of everybody's time if two actors are in front practicing drama and language skills, while twenty-eight are sitting at their desks being entertained. It's great entertainment; it's lousy education.

To maximize the value of the exercise, the fun and the content standards in the activity, we need to find ways to engage every student. The self-confident and focused student isn't a problem, but we have to find ways to engage the student with a Ph.D. in shyness. No one escapes in the war on ignorance. Even if they desperately want to escape.

There are two ways I check for non-involvement on the most superficial level. First of all, I predict which students will resist learning and participating. Maybe once you get to know them, you can put all your students into this matrix below.

Students who:	Want to perform	Do not want to perform
Want to learn	Group A	Group B
Do not want to learn	Group C	Group D

Group A is one that I don't have to worry about; in fact, that's the group you usually don't even have to "teach." You just mention the content once, and they get it.

Group B students can be won over without much effort. They are nervous about having to get up and do stuff (desks are safe). But these are good students; they just prefer the passive, non-threatening mode of learning. Once the tone of the class and the activities are officially safe and fun, these kids shift quite easily to group A types.

Group C has an immature nature. Many times these are the boys who are playful, physical and social, but who don't like to do paperwork or think. They like to play (because they have the mindset of nine- to twelve-year-olds), but learning isn't fun nor is it cool. But if the games are fun to play, and they need the learning to play and win (competition is a *carrot* here), they will learn because it's part of the game (so it's not *real* learning).

Group D is the crew that separates the magical teacher from the functioning teacher. If I'm ever successful in winning over or engaging a group D student, I know that I have done something of quality as a teacher. These are the quiet or obnoxiously loud, very passive or very disruptive students. This kid is easy to ignore or resent. You forget that the quiet kid even exists. The obnoxious disrupter makes every effort you undertake twice as energy-draining. With both types, I think, it's just fear controlling their behavior. Everyone would like to be smart and would like the world to know it. So, fear and weak self-concept are the obstacles.

The last distracter from achieving my educational objectives is the evil twin of the method itself: entertainment. Watching an engaging drama or comedy will capture the attention of the class, which looks like learning to the dilettante, but it doesn't mean that students are improving their memory of something, clarifying a concept or improving a skill. It just shows the enchantment of entertainment. And kids get enough of that at home or elsewhere.

What follows are some scenarios to help you with ideas for safely involving every student. With the first approaches (scenarios one and two), the strategies serve needs by what you can see: most kids are just watching, and shy kids look as though they want to melt into the floor. The second approach lists some strategies based on the learning scaffold: first, facts; second, concepts; third, skills and applications. You might read all of them if you have time, or you can just scan the headings and read the ones that seem to fit situations you recognize.

Most Kids Are Just Being Entertained

Scenario one: Two students are performing, and twenty-eight are just watching.

Strategy one — Set up teams

You might start with two teams but four or six might be better. Just the use of competition makes the "stakes" higher. This strategy, coupled with the fact that each student will eventually have to get up and do something, makes accountability a motivating factor. Keep in mind that the competition element is only to improve the personal "cost" for each student, not in the end to produce one winning group and one or more losers.

Strategy two — "You might be next"

Jane Shaffer told me this strategy several years ago. While one group is about to perform, tell the opposing team, "I will pick one (or two) of you to compete next at the same activity." Now this fact may be as obvious as air to everybody, but it reminds the observers that their turn is coming. The effect is observable as they watch for *content and "how to"* rather than the entertainment value of the actions. They are focused on the learning objective rather than the activity used to reinforce the objective.

If the two competing teams are focused, I might look at the two to four teams making up the audience and tell them, "now two of the teams in the audience are next. I'll pick you in just a minute." Again, this is obvious to everyone, but now the two performing teams are test cases the audience can privately learn from or test themselves against. I might catch the eye of, and smile at, a couple of students I know are fearful to let them know that everyone's important, and that I will be supportive.

Side note: If while the two on-stage teams are performing, I note audience members talking in earnest with each other, the noise possibly disruptive to the performers, I can respond in two ways. One, if I'm teaching theatre etiquette, I will address the behavior during or after the performance. Two, if I'm teaching a content standard from English, I will let the "chatter" continue because the chatter is one or more students processing the content of the performers, possibly in preparation for their performance. In the second case, what looks like disruptive behavior is learning and processing. Maybe I can't get the kids to do homework to practice important learning, so I need to be able to recognize what constructive behavior in class looks like or I might quiet the students when they are most pointedly addressing the work I want.

Strategy three — Audience team judging (consensus)

Make the audience members the judges for evaluating performance work of the two competing teams. If you have the audience applaud loudest for the team that did the best, you never really know what they are cheering for (Popularity? Entertainment? Who knows?). If the audience is composed of several soon-to-be competing teams, have the separate teams confer privately and come to consensus on their votes. First tell them the criteria (content standard demonstration) for the voting. Tell them that you will choose one member of each audience team to declare the group's finding and to explain what their thinking was. Catch eyes with the shiest of kids to let them know that they might be the one required to declare the team's choice.

Don't let the groups choose their own spokesperson; you can guess who will be chosen and who will not. That allows passive people off the hook. Don't say whom you will choose to speak for each group so each student thinks "it might be me."

Strategy four — Opposing team members individually write the errors made during the opposing team's performance

Say the opposing team sends two members up. One states the parts of speech, one at a time. After each is stated by actor A, actor B has to give an example. To keep the opposing team focused on the knowledge and skills the lesson is targeting, have each member, with his own piece of paper, write down any parts of speech that are repeated or left out (error), or any examples given that are incorrect (for "preposition," actor B gives "and" as the example). Once the competing team is done with its round, have the opposing team put down their pencils and check their notes. If fifty percent or more of the

114

team's paperwork has the same errors listed, then that team gets points for identifying errors.

You can have all the audience groups do the same thing and earn "savings" points which can be used the next time they compete.

Strategy five — Audience challenge

This is very similar to what is described in strategy four. Two teams compete and judges evaluate on errors and points. The audience teams can confer and come to consensus on any errors the competing teams made that were not picked up and noted by the judges. They might be something like back-up judges. *(Note: Speaking as a judge, I periodically miss an error [or correct response] by a performer. Sometimes the pace is too fast to pick up everything.)*

Strategy six — Multi-group tasks

See "Scavenger Hunt II", game 104, in the New Games section. A paragraph is projected on the wall and papers with the paragraph are handed to all members of all groups (who compete at the same time). Each member is to do the task (i.e., count the number of verbs, adverbs and interjections) and write the numbers on lines at the bottom of their papers *in ink*. Once all have done that privately, groups have one minute to confer on their answers, decide what the correct numbers are, and then fill in their group choices of numbers *in ink* at the bottom of a group paper. All group papers (all individual and the one group paper with totals agreed upon by consensus) are collected. The judge or emcee counts all the correct scores in each group packet (individual and group papers). The number of correct scores in the packet is the team's score.

This format makes the individual and the group accountable. It allows for individual thinking and for group conferencing and processing on the content knowledge. The game and the group apply pressure for accountability, not just the teacher.

Scenario two: The super-shy student who conveys, "I can't (won't) do this."

Strategy one — Let them observe only

Allow the kid to sit out for some games, rounds or days. Give the signal that says, "I know it's scary. There's no rush."

Strategy two — Let the shy kid be a judge (power)
This makes the kid think "I'm not performing" though she is operating as a part of the structure. If the student judges accurately, you know she is processing the content, and that is the goal. Education wins. If the class is a drama class, then you have two choices: encourage her to perform later once she feels more comfortable and has seen that performing is safe or make her deliver the judgment with an authoritative tone (emotional presentation) so that she is demonstrating some drama elements.

Strategy three — Let the shy student honk for errors (power)
If you are playing "Scene without a Letter," for example, put the shy student off-stage with a horn to honk every time one of the performers speaks a word with the taboo letter in it. The non-performer is contributing, processing the English content (spelling), identifying errors, and helping the vulnerability and entertainment of the exercise. If yours is an English class, those results sound pretty good.

Strategy four — Let the shy student be the spokesperson for the audience group that challenges the performers' "answers"
The shy student has to listen to the group discussion and then announce the decision of the audience team. It's a dynamic contribution that doesn't take place on the "stage" so it feels safer.

Strategy five — Use the shy student only as a part of a team in a group activity
The shy student will feel safe, for example, as a part of the guessing teammates in "What's in a Minute." Even safer, the shy student can work with one or more partners in a written activity, such as "Scavenger Hunt." Several games do not require a team member to perform alone; these are the safe choices for the shiest students.

Strategy six — Have the shy student prepare materials for a competition
This approach saves time and labor for the teacher, gives the shy student safety and power, and allows the teacher to discuss and assess

this student's learning. Choose a game that requires materials that have not been seen by any player on either team. For example, "Scavenger Hunt" requires a paper with a paragraph at the top of a page and an overhead projector transparency of the same for use in the game. Furthermore, there needs to be an "answer sheet" with the correct number of each item identified for the "hunt." The shy student can prepare both, working with the teacher prior to the competition to make sure the materials are usable and the answer sheet is accurate. This student gets one-on-one contact, and he might be the judge and counter of correct answers in the competition — power and prestige. If any answers are challenged by the competing team, this shy student is now the authority and the first to clarify why the correct answers are correct.

The Learning Scaffold

Teachers must be careful not to ask students too quickly to go from their desks to performance activities. Such a big jump can produce frustration or confusion for the students when they are standing in front of the class. It's a good idea to start them at their desks alone or with a supporting partner working with the new information. At this stage, it is also good to give them the littlest bits of information rather than whole chunks. For example, instead of asking them to memorize the eights parts of speech and present all of them with mimed actions to the class, you might ask them to do the same with only two or three of the easiest parts of speech. Start them on the first and easiest *rung* of the ladder so that they feel safe and the chances for success are high. Then they can climb up with tasks that are more complex or challenging.

Teaching Knowledge and Facts

Strategy one — Start with writing activities at desks

If you set this up well, all kids — even the shiest — get to hear, see, write and talk about the knowledge/facts that are needed to move to skills and applications. The desks are safe zones where kids can control who sees what.

Strategy two — Progressive group sizes going from large to small to solo

Once kids have had a chance to work the knowledge alone, consider putting them in large groups to continue processing the knowledge. By large I mean big enough that the shiest kids can hide a bit and observe if needed.

With the next task, or the same activity repeated, make the groups smaller so the need to participate increases with the number of times the students have worked with the targeted facts. The final phase in this strategy is to get the kids working in pairs or alone with confidence. If the sequence of activities is smooth and the amount of repetition is sufficient, most, or all, students should feel that the facts are well embedded in their heads.

Here's a simple sample sequence:

Facts to memorize: ten vocabulary words

Activity one (private and written): "Copy the words onto your paper."

Activity two (large groups of five students): "As a group come up with movements that you all do at the same time in the space by your desks that communicates the definition of each word."

Activity three (small groups of three students): "Write a short story or paragraph using all ten of the vocabulary words. Standing up by your desks, read the paragraph aloud to the class, each of the groups' members reading one sentence at a time."

Activity four (duet): "After practicing at your desks, present a conversation with your partner to the class, using all ten words in sentences correctly. If you write out the conversation with the vocabulary words, you may read it if you want when presenting to the class."

Strategy three — Timed lists (large to small groups)

Note: The following describes the activity sequence with the students standing in front of the class reciting the vocabulary words. All of these activities, however, can also be done with more "safety" by having the groups write on paper instead of speak up front. Knowing your class of students, where might you begin to develop fun and safety?

This strategy might feel a lot like strategy two above, and it is. The difference is that there's more pressure here with the stopwatch and the performance activity. I like this activity, because I've seen it work well, getting kids to memorize words quickly while having fun. (Side note: When I first started using this technique a couple of years ago, one thing that struck me was how the students retained the terms weeks after the initial game was played.) I can't tell if this game is cruel, but it's so much fun that no one seems to care.

Set-up: Show the list of targeted words on an overhead for maybe ten seconds telling the group that you are going to ask two people to recall all the words. Pick a few victims to come up and try. They will most likely not get all the words, so encourage their efforts to try and get the class to applaud.

Activity one (large group): Break the class into fours or fives. Tell them that each group will come up and recite the list from memory within fifteen seconds. Show the list and watch them strategize (i.e., each memorizes only two words, etc.). Call each group up one at a time. They face the class while the overhead transparency is viewed by the audience (they can be judges and find success and errors — processing the words again and again, preparing for their own turn).

Activity two (small group): In pairs the students are to prepare to recite the words from memory in the shortest time possible. "We will keep the pairs' times on the board." (During the recitation, remind the students that the speed doesn't matter; it's the memorizing of the terms that's the goal.)

Activity three (individual performance in small group [with cheating]): In pairs the team will compete after practicing at desks. The difference is that one member of each pair recites the ten while timed and the time is recorded. The second member does the same and the times are added together. Cheating is allowed: if the reciting member forgets one or more words, and the partner knows it, the latter can whisper the missing words to the performer. Remember, the activity is to produce memorization, not to produce a grade to put in the grade book. The cheating whisper comes from a teammate, "a friend who's helping me," and helps make it fun, friendly and safe. Team building will pay off a thousand times later on.

As always, if you have super-shy students, turn them into judges or have them control the "check-off" sheet as each group performs so that someone officially knows if all terms have been recited.

Teaching Concepts

Say that one way or another, you've gotten the students to where they recognize the essential terms and possibly can recite definitions. This only means they've memorized the terms and definitions; they probably don't understand them all.

Concept: "a generalized idea of a class of objects." (Webster's New World Dictionary, 1985).

I teach acting, and one of the terms my students need to memorize is "focus." If they say the term ("focus") and define it in its simplest form ("where the audience's attention is drawn"), I know they've memorized the facts. For beginning actors, however, I can pretty much guarantee that they don't understand the concept, which is broader, more encompassing, than the definition. In the concept (the "idea"), there are many contributing terms and skills (body and stage positions, stage pictures, storytelling, etc.). My task is to get them to an introductory level of understanding the concept: Focus, like the lens of a camera, points the audience to actions, gestures and statements that reveal character, meaning and motivation that are intended to affect the audience towards certain thoughts or feelings. That is a bit more than the initial definition, "where the audience's attention is drawn." To *understand* the concept more fully, they need to experience terms and explore examples.

So where do we begin teaching *concepts*?

Strategy one — "What's in a Minute," and "What's in a Minute II"

This game is a form of charades, but check the description to get a picture of how it's set up. The list of "whats" to communicate without regular speech forces the players and audience to understand the terms and definitions from another angle, here through actions and possibly creative metaphors. To continue with the example of "focus" above, the performer might try to convey the term by suggesting two actors on a stage and a director who makes minor adjustments in their body positions until he is delighted with which actor dominates the two-person scene. For a metaphor, the performer might imitate a photographer adjusting the lens of a camera until it's perfect, a scientist with a microscope being adjusted or a pirate with one of those long telescopes.

The point is to force an explanation without the normal word definition. Perhaps alone or in pairs, students should try to draw the concept or write a song lyric to explain it.

Strategy one A — "What's in a Minute" (shy students)
Shy kids won't call out choices if other students are aggressive, louder and willing to play. So run the game with an elimination. Make teams of eleven if the list to be performed has ten items on it. The performing team member tries to do the list one item at a time. The ten guessing members guess, but after one has guessed a correct answer, she must separate from the group, leaving nine guessers. This continues until the last guesser is the only one to guess the last of the ten "whats" from the list. Shy students might be motivated by the elimination to guess earlier to avoid being the last guesser.

Strategy two — "What's in a Minute II" (shy students)
If you know you have a shy student who might not participate well with the elimination described above, make the shy kid the performer's coach. Read the description of "What's in a Minute II." Have the shy student help the performer with ideas that do not repeat any of the devices used in the "What's in a Minute" round just played. The job gives the shy student creative power, she works the concepts (which is the point), and this allows her to avoid the limelight. (Praise the ideas for this round so the coach looks brilliant after the round is over.)

Strategy three — "What's in a Minute II" (multiple groups)
Picture this. Around the room are student groups of four. At each group's table is a judge for that group only. In front of the room stands one actor to do the charades for "What's in a Minute II" for all of the student groups at the same time. Here is the difference: there is no calling out loud of the guesses. Each team privately confers on the correct answer, comes to consensus and writes down their answer on paper. The judge for each group looks at the written answer, and if it is correct calls "correct." When two groups have their answers judged

as "correct," the performer goes to the next word on the list and the process continues until all ten "whats" have been communicated. This game is somewhat private and allows partners to discuss the concepts communicated by the performer. If you have super-shy students, let them be judges and praise their work after the competition.

Strategy four — "What's in a Minute II" (preparation only)

Divide the students into pairs. Distribute the list of already memorized and defined terms. Give the teams a workable time limit to brainstorm and record as many ways to communicate the concepts as they can devise as if they were about to play "What's in a Minute II." Remind them that the presentation ideas can use mime, gibberish, sound effects and melodies. Credit will not be given for performing the ideas, but simply for coming up with the most ideas for each concept that the pairs can. Each team simply explains the ideas with the group to present the concepts in multiple ways. .

Teaching Skills and Applications

Many of the games presented in this text and in *Grammar Wars* require the students to practice and demonstrate skills in language or drama. In fact, to my taste, the best performance games are the ones that rely on the students knowing the facts and having some proficiency with the concepts and skills. With all that under their belts, then we get to see scene work that adds to the entertainment value of the improv work.

Because this section is to illustrate **how to practice** skills and **apply** them to real language contexts, I will only use two games ("Scavenger Hunt" and "Scene without a _____") to help you see the process.

Strategy one — "Scavenger Hunt" (written process)

(This was described earlier.)

The description below fits a lesson that targets the students' skill of identifying parts of speech, specifically adverbs, conjunctions and prepositions.

The class is divided into trios. Every student in every group gets the paper with the paragraph, the items to be identified and counted, and the lines at the bottom where students will write the totals they've counted in the writing (see sample format in the Appendices). The first task is for all students to do the activity privately, writing their totals on the lines at the bottom of the page in ink so the answers cannot be changed. With their papers in hand, the trios meet away from other groups to review their answers, agree on what's correct, solve confusion about correct and incorrect choices and finally record the totals they agree upon as a group by consensus. They put the group's final choices of totals on a new, fourth paper. All four papers are stapled and handed in to a judge who gives a point for the correct individual and group totals at the bottom of each page.

The students think alone, think as a group, privately get to confer and evaluate their choices and thinking, and the results are somehow made public, but who specifically made errors isn't clear so there is some safety.

Strategy two — "Scavenger Hunt" (performance)

This is a more advanced form of the game and requires students to feel safe or to be pretty good with the skill of identifying the parts of speech in the example above (or whatever you're trying to get the kids to do).

Preparation

Still in trios, each group prepares a three-sentence paragraph (or three separate unrelated sentences). The teacher will choose the parts of speech that will be targeted for the skill development (say, adverbs, conjunctions and prepositions as in the example above). On their papers they are to have marked all the examples of the target parts of speech with the correct totals at the bottom of the page.

Memory Version

The emcee collects the paragraph/sentence samples with the correct answers and calls up the first trio to perform. Each of the trio members is assigned one of the parts of speech. As the sentences are read slowly (possibly twice), the performers count the number of times their specific part of speech showed up. At the end of the reading of the sentences, each player calls the total of times his part of speech showed up in the three-sentence set.

Consensus Version

The three-sentence paragraphs are converted to transparencies and the sentences are projected onto the screen. The competing team confers on the number of times each part of speech shows up. Possibly they are marking adverbs with a green pen, conjunctions with red and prepositions with black. The totals are assembled by consensus. Points are scored for correct totals.

This form is good, because the other groups, while not competing, are working with the projected text, looking for errors in the performing team's work, all the while practicing the targeted skill.

Strategy three — "Scene without a _____" (i.e., preposition)
Horn Form

The first form of this game uses only two actors. Both are on-stage and given the basics for an improvised scene. They are also given a part of speech that is taboo that must never be used or the error horn will honk requiring the erring actor to revise the last-spoken line. The emcee says that prepositions cannot be used and the scene begins. If a preposition shows up the horn honks and the lines are revised. Judges count the errors each actor makes in the time limit and the actor with the fewest errors wins.

Elimination Form

Two teams each send up three actors. Each team's actors number themselves 1, 2, and 3. The 1 actors from each team go on-stage for a two-person scene derived from an idea from the audience. The taboo part of speech (or whatever) is given by the audience. The scene begins. With this version, when an error is made and the horn honks, the erring actor exits to the wings and the teammate with the next number enters and repairs the line to omit the taboo part of speech, and the scene continues. The rotation can go on and on, or the scene can end with a time limit. Possibly, each actor is allowed on-stage only once. In a straight elimination format, the team whose actor remains on-stage after all the opponents have been eliminated wins.

Chapter 6
Basic Mime

To produce good improv, actors should be in control of some basic mime technique. I don't mean that you have to study with Marcel Marceau by any means (though if you get the chance ...). There are a couple of very simple basics that can help you with manual (hand) illusions, emotional value and creating space.

Because you go onto the stage with nothing, nothing is there — except maybe some rehearsal furniture. So basically you're on your own, and all you've got is you. With a little bit of technique and imagination, your body, face and voice are sufficient to create anything you want or need. If your technique is clear enough, the audience will see where you are and what you're doing. If you care about what you see and those things "change" you (Johnstone says the audience pays to see characters change), then the audience will care. And if you can do that, well then, you're an actor!

Manual Illusions

Hand-created illusions are created initially through "the rule of contrast." Throw a round tomato toward a brick wall. It's round as can be while it's in the air, but when the wall shows up, *Wham!* The tomato is suddenly, and I want you to see the *suddenly,* flat. In a split second, its shape changes. That's the timing needed to perform the rule of contrast.

The contrast itself is really simple. There are two basic shapes for the mime's hand to make: flat and round (or "soft"). Try it where you are: hold the book with one hand. Make your free hand flat (spread the fingers apart a little). Check to see if the fingers, palm and heel all line up on one single plane (as much as possible). That's flat. Now to make the round ("soft") hand, just relax a bit, and your hand should shift into a soft curve or arc (fingers together or side-by-side).

Let's practice. When I tell you "flat," you flatten the hand. When I next say "round," you relax and let it form a soft curve. OK?

"Flat; round; flat; round; flat; round; flat; round; flat; round; flat; round; flat; round; flat; round; flat; round; flat; round; flat; round; flat; round; flat; round; flat; round; flat; round; flat; round; flat; round." Now you are either an expert mime, or your hand and arm muscles are so tight from needless over-exertion that you're convulsing.

So let's move along and assume that with time you can go back and forth between flat and round without your muscles tweaking out on you. All shapes can be divided into two categories: flat and round. A wall (the average one) is flat. A ball is round. A tabletop is flat. Keys are round (think of contacting the imaginary keys with just your thumb and index finger in a pinch. See that? Well, between flat and round, it sure isn't flat! So it's round.) Cabinet doors are flat. Doorknobs are round. The side of an elephant is flat (just trust me here). A peanut is round. And so it goes.

So the "rule of contrast" says if the object I'm going to create is a door (flat), I have to **start with a contrasting shape,** round. If I'm going to hold an apple (round), the rule of contrast says, start flat. It's that simple for the initial contact, the "take."

When you're done with the object/illusion, you need to "release" it, and you do that by the same rule. If you're holding a round apple, when you set it down or throw it into the air, your hand goes flat to show the release. When you are done with the door surface or cabinet surface, you change your hand shape to round ("soft") to show the release. It's that simple for when you let go, the "release."

You've got the "rule of contrast" going on with your hands now. That's good. The next simple skill to get control of is the "snap." The tomato when it hits the flat, brick wall changes shape in a tenth of a second, so the shift from a round to a flat hand should happen with a split-second change — "contact!" Similarly, the release to a round hand should be instantaneous once the flat surface has been released. "Snap on; snap off!" Why? Crisp takes and releases convey the shapes of hard illusions; soft takes and releases suggest mushy materials (pillows, rubber walls, soft bellies, etc.).

In classic French technique there is a "toc" that occurs in the mime's torso that conveys the reaction to the object being created. It's sudden, because the object has qualities that make the character react, that change the character, that engage the character as somebody that develops interest from the audience. The "snap" described above has the same sense of change, but not necessarily the emotional quality. Sometimes, a glass of water is just a glass and not the essence of a scene.

Illusions by Avoidance

This doesn't have the same quality of creating a specific object, but it's useful so I want to include it here. Oftentimes you want to initiate your work with an object, not by clearly creating it so the audience immediately knows what it is. You might be walking across the stage and duck your head just in time, and then watch the "object" trail off to the side wondering, "now who put that there?" The initial mystery in the audience's minds, "what was that?," can engage their minds in questions and answers and keep them following you. Even if you never identify the object to avoid, if the actor were to go about his business walking back and forth, each time having to duck, that might be the most interesting aspect of the scene. Put five things to avoid in the location while the mime is crossing back and forth from the refrigerator to the counter, simply trying to finish making a peanut butter and jelly sandwich. The avoidance "obstacle course" would be the heart of the scene, yet the mime never actually *takes* or *releases* any of the most important illusions.

Creating Space (When You've Got Just a Little)

You might see two willing actors being given a scene to do where the characters have to give the impression of walking in a great open space (a park, downtown, etc.) in a classroom or on a stage. Off they go walking away down stage (so the audience can see them), and in four steps they are either into a row of desks, or they are walking off the edge of the stage into the empty orchestra pit.

They were told to walk, so they walked. "We did what you told us," but now you have to fill out an accident report. So, it's time to have a mannered walk, or a way to suggest a walk that is acceptable to the audience.

127

Walk in an easy circle, and when you come around to an open position facing the audience, show what you need to show next in order to move the story along (discover a new room, an engaging poodle, a pile of poodles, a poodle pile, whatever). Accompany this with a facial expression and neck work that suggests that you are looking at significant distances. If you "see" someone you know, speak with greater-than-normal volume. Once you see something or someone of interest, walk in a straight line, even if your volume suggested twenty yards while your straight-line steps suggested ten feet. The audience will give that "space warp" to you.

Manipulation

When I first heard of this three-phase technique, I thought, "yeah, OK, so what?" But when you watch someone working this well, audiences are sucked into the action.

The **approach** precedes the **take**. The character is just moving along, doing an action or walking in a routine fashion. Suddenly, she sees something in the location and possibly stops. She considers the object carefully with an escalating tone (fascination, love, curiosity, etc.). She moves toward it, possibly away, and back toward it again. Regardless, you know she's going to "get" it.

The **take** is the second action, which was described earlier. The actor snaps the **take,** and/or with the "toc" from the abdomen suggests the object's effect on the character. Imagine, a character is walking along despondently, sees the most amazing flower and makes the **approach**. She is curious in the final moment of the **approach** and does the **take**. (The flower is "round" so the hand starts flat and snaps to a round — pinch the index finger to the thumb to make the illusion light and feminine.)

The character does whatever she might with the flower (putting it in the lapel, hair, replanting it lovingly back in the ground, etc.) and then performs the **release** with a reverse finger snap that ends the manual work with the illusion. Certainly, because the engagement with the spectacular flower changed the character, after the release while exiting, she will probably look back at the flower in the ground or stop to raise the lapel so that the flower can be smelled just before the end of the scene.

Approach, take, release.

Hopefully, the skills and concepts described above seem simple and manageable with practice. With improv and Grammar Wars, actors will need anything at any time, and good, basic mime skills will communicate the objects and the relationships between objects and characters in a wonderfully entertaining way.

Chapter 7
Vertical Standards Strings

Using Standards Strand Ladders

Teachers around the country are at various stages of using or converting to the use of standards prescribed either by national, state or local educational organizations. The activity I've seen is a reading of the documents and an initial despair that comes over the teachers when the scope and breadth of the document is encountered. "How can I teach all I am supposed to teach in a single year?!"

The shock is understandable because the documents do a pretty good job of prescribing essential elements of each field presented. There is a lot to teach and little time. Next to those facts is the reality of how slow the learning process is even when one has a group of students who are willing to learn.

So how does each teacher wisely and economically do the job so that progress results?

While the standards documents help, they don't easily give us all the information we need. So we have some work to do on our own. This chapter is designed to help you see how you can work "vertically" with your school and district to achieve essential K-12 final proficiencies in all of your students.

As I've gone over the standards for California, alone and with colleagues, I've concluded that the standards are not all-inclusive and self-evident. What does that mean? You have to know about your field in order to know what the standards are stating. You have to be able to do a thorough task analysis of each standard and the performance standards stated or implied in order to know how to diagnostically test and teach the standard.

Example: A few years back, in order to prepare to teach a group of teachers at College of the Siskiyous in Weed, California, I targeted the lesson on using Grammar Wars to model teaching a two-hour lesson on the development of understanding and of the skills necessary to identify active and passive voice and to be able to convert passive to active structures.

I went to the standards to identify the seventh grade standard for active and passive voice. I then looked at the kindergarten through sixth grade standards to see what standards preceded seventh grade that were needed to prepare students for this seventh grade instruction. I found items in kindergarten through fifth grade, and nothing obvious in sixth grade. (See Standards String for Active and Passive Voice in the Appendices.) That told me that each teacher in kindergarten through fifth grade needed to know what knowledge, concepts and skills to produce in those grades to make the seventh grade teacher's job manageable. It also told me that the sixth grade teacher needed to understand her job to repeat and reinforce all the kindergarten through fifth grade learning so that nothing was forgotten when the students arrived in seventh grade. Vertical teamwork!

Without a local awareness of the specific proficiencies to be developed in later grades, teachers may not know how to teach or focus the teaching on a required grade-level standard. In the California standards, second grade teachers are to teach students to "identify and correctly use various parts of speech, including nouns and verbs ... " In third grade teachers are to teach students to "identify and use past, present and future verb tenses ... " Grade four teachers are to teach students to "identify and use ... irregular verbs ... " Here's my point: if the earlier grade teachers know what the essential proficiencies are for upper grades, they will know how to prudently focus their instruction at their grade level.

The seventh grade teacher, teaching active and passive voice skills, needs kids to arrive knowing all nine forms of "to be" in all the tenses. A teacher who knows how she fits in to the vertical curriculum knows what's essential and what's secondary. A teacher who does not understand her place in a vertical team may, with an interest in developing vocabulary, only work with less common verbs to widen the student's accessible vocabulary. There's nothing wrong with that, but if everybody knows what's essential later on, they know what must be included and what can be included but not prioritized. It's about priorities and focus in a world of limited time.

Point? If kids arrive with competency in parts of speech and high proficiency with the irregular verb "to be," then the seventh grade teacher need only teach participles (present and past forms) and active and passive voices, as the standards expect.

The standards strand ladders in this chapter set up by my colleague Joe Bell try to establish the vertical standards strings that lead to some essential proficiencies for our state's high school students. Teachers at various grade levels can see the proficiencies for high school students and where and how their grade standards fit in.

To the right of each level are Grammar Wars games and exercises that are appropriate for the grade level learning described, what to teach and the exercises to teach it. These games are found in *Grammar Wars: 179 games and improvs for learning language arts*. Based on your familiarity with your unique students, feel free to modify any games and exercises to make them simpler, to ensure success, or to make them more challenging to stretch and challenge the students as they reinforce and apply the knowledge concepts and skills.

Strand Ladder #1

Proficiency: Written and Oral English Language Conventions
✔ Students will be able to correctly use commas for subordinating and coordinating conjunctions.

Previous skills needed:
✔ Subject, predicate, conjunctions, clauses
✔ Sentence types: simple, compound, complex and compound/complex
✔ Sentence kinds: interrogative, declarative, imperative and exclamatory

Grade	Standard	Activity, game number
9/10	1.1 Identify and correctly use commas between two independent clauses joined by a conjunction.	Turret Trade-off, 149 Voice-Over with Punctuation, 90 Sentence Charade, 94 Name That Sentence, 93 Pyramid Story, 103 Sentence Scramble, 157 Stand and Deliver, 68 Scene with ..., 76
8	1.1 Use varied sentence types, subordination and coordination. 1.4 Use correct punctuation.	Comma Along with Me, 82 Four-Sentence Scene, 95 Junior Sentence Types, 101 Name That Sentence, 93
7	1.4 Demonstrate mechanics of writing (e.g., quotation marks, commas at end of dependent clauses).	Start and Stop, 77 Quotes, 83 Punctuate Your Neighbor, 81 Punctuate This, 78 Punctuation Ballet, 79

6	1.1 Use varied sentence types. Use effective coordination/ subordination of ideas.	Half Thought/Whole Thought, 98 Junior Sentence Type, 101 Name That Sentence, 93
5	1.1 Identify and use independent and dependent clauses.	Name That Sentence, 93 Half Thought/Whole Thought, 98 Junior Sentence Type, 101
4	1.1 Use simple and compound sentences. 1.3 Identify and use coordinating conjunctions.	Name That Sentence, 93 Half Thought/Whole Thought, 98
3	1.1 Understand and use sentence kinds. 1.2 Identify subjects and verbs in agreement.	Junior Sentence Type, 101 Name That Sentence, 93 Half Thought/Whole Thought, 98
2	1.1 Distinguish between complete and incomplete sentences.	Name That Sentence, 93 Half Thought/Whole Thought, 98 Junior Sentence Type, 101
1	1.1 Write and speak in complete, coherent sentences. 1.4 Distinguish between declarative, exclamatory and interrogative sentences.	Half Thought/Whole Thought, 98 Junior Sentence Type, 101 Name That Sentence, 93
K	1.1 Recognize and use complete, coherent sentences when speaking.	Half Thought/Whole Thought, 98 Junior Sentence Type, 101

Strand Ladder #2

Proficiency: Written and Oral English Language Conventions
✔ Students will demonstrate knowledge of pronoun/antecedent agreement.

Previous skills needed:
✔ Understanding of pronouns, nouns, case, singular and plural nouns, antecedent

Grade	Standard	Activity, game number
9/10	1.3 Demonstrate an understanding of proper English usage and control of grammar.	Edit It!, 153 This Part Only!, 56 Scene without ..., 76 Parts Expert, 60 Parts Idiot, 61
8	1.4 Edit written manuscripts to ensure that correct grammar is used.	Get Back in Line!, 104 Edit It!, 153 Alpha-Parts, 73 Dropout I and II, 57, 58
7	1.2 Make clear references between pronouns and antecedents. 1.3 Identify all parts of speech. 1.4 Demonstrate appropriate English usage.	Edit It!, 153 Alpha-Parts, 73 Dropout I and II, 57, 58 Get Back in Line!, 104
6	1.2 Identify and properly use indefinite pronouns and verb tenses.	Get Back in Line!, 104 Edit It!, 153

5	1.2 Identify and correctly use pronouns.	Get Back in Line!, 104 Edit It!, 153
4	1.0 Students write and speak with a command of standard English conventions appropriate to this grade level.	Get Back in Line!, 104 Edit It!, 153
3	1.2 Identify and use pronouns correctly in speaking and writing.	Get Back in Line!, 104 Edit It!, 153
2	1.3 Identify and use parts of speech in writing and speaking.	Get Back in Line!, 104 Edit It!, 153
1	1.2 Identify and correctly use plural and singular nouns. 1.3 Identify and use pronouns.	Get Back in Line!, 104 Edit It!, 153
K	1.1 Recognize and use coherent sentences when speaking.	Edit It!, 153 Get Back in Line!, 104

Strand Ladder #3

Proficiency: Listening and Speaking
✔ Students will be able to deliver an oral, persuasive argument to an intended audience.

Previous skills needed:
✔ Grade-level vocabulary
✔ Tone
✔ Reasoning

Grade	Standard	Activity, game number
9/10	2.5 Deliver persuasive arguments. 2.5.a Structure ideas and arguments coherently and logically. 2.5.c Clarify and defend positions with precise and relevant evidence. 2.5.d Anticipate and address the listeners' concerns and counterarguments.	Bad Ad, 145 Adverts, 143
8	1.3 Organize information for a purpose. Match tone to audience and purpose.	Adverts, 143 Bad Ad, 145 Give Me Your Tone!, 139 Story, Story, Out, 136 Sounds Like, 18
7	1.4 Organize information for a purpose. 1.5 Arrange details in relation to audience.	Adverts, 143 Bad Ad, 145 Give Me Your Tone!, 139

6	1.4 Select focus, organization and point of view to match purpose. 1.7 Use effective rate, volume, pitch, tone and nonverbal elements.	Adverts, 143 Bad Ad, 145 Chores, 110 Getting a Rise, 133
5	1.4 Select focus, organization and point of view. 1.6 Appropriate verbal cues, facial expressions, gestures.	Adverts, 143 Bad Ad, 145 Chores, 110
4	1.5 Give effective introductions and conclusions. 1.6 Use traditional structures.	Adverts, 143 Bad Ad, 145 Chores, 110
3	1.1 Retell what has been said by a speaker. 1.5 Organize ideas chronologically. 1.7 Use vocabulary to establish tone.	Chores, 110 Finish Your Plate, 33
2	1.3 Paraphrase information that has been shared. 1.5 Organize presentation to maintain focus. 1.6 Speak clearly at an appropriate pace.	Chores, 110

1	1.2 Ask questions for clarification and understanding. 1.3 Give, restate, follow simple two-step directions. 1.4 Stay on topic when speaking. 1.5 Use descriptive words when speaking.	Chores, 110
K	1.1 Follow one- and two-step oral directions. 1.2 Share information and ideas in complete, coherent sentences. 2.3 Relate an experience in logical sequence.	Chores, 110

Strand Ladder #4

Proficiency: Fact Versus Opinion
✔ Students will understand and identify the difference between fact and opinion and use both effectively in their writing.

Previous skills needed:
✔ Understanding of evidence, opinion, fact, defend, precise language
✔ Grade-level reading skills

Grade	Standard	Activity, game number
9/10	*Reading* 2.8 Evaluate an author's argument by critiquing generalizations and evidence. *Writing* 1.4 Develop main ideas with evidence. 2.3a Use evidence to support thesis. 2.4c Defend positions with facts, opinions, quotations.	Bad Ad, 145 Edit It!, 153 Why'd It Happen?, 113 In Your Own Words, 114 Speed Reader, 115 Ears and Actions, 122
8	*Reading* 3.7 Analyze literature for attitudes of author. *Writing* 2.4b Differentiate fact from opinion.	Bad Ad, 145 Edit It!, 153

7	*Reading* 2.6 Assess the author's evidence for claims. *Writing* 1.2 Support all statements and claims with facts and examples.	Bad Ad, 145 Edit It!, 153
6	*Reading* 2.8 Notice instances of unsupported inferences, fallacious reasoning and propaganda in text. *Writing* 2.2d Offer evidence to validate arguments.	Bad Ad, 145 Edit It!, 153
5	*Reading* 2.5 Distinguish facts, supported inferences and opinions in text. 2.3 Discern, identify, assess evidence. *Writing* 2.3c Develop topic with simple facts.	Bad Ad, 145 Edit It!, 153
4	*Reading* 2.4 Evaluate new information. 2.6 Distinguish between fact and opinion. *Writing* 1.2c Include supporting paragraphs with facts.	Bad Ad, 145 Edit It!, 153

3	*Reading* 2.2 Locate information in a text. *Writing* 1.1 Include supporting facts in a paragraph.	Edit It!, 153 Why'd It Happen?, 113 In Your Own Words, 114 Speed Reader, 115
2	*Reading* 2.5 Restate facts and details in the text to clarify and organize ideas.	Edit It!, 153 Why'd It Happen?, 113 In Your Own Words, 114 Speed Reader, 115 Ears and Actions, 122
1	*Reading* 2.1 Identify logical order in text. 2.5 Confirm predictions in a text. 2.7 Retell the central ideas in passages.	Edit It!, 153 Why'd It Happen?, 113 In Your Own Words, 114 Speed Reader, 115
K	*Reading* 1.3 Understand that printed materials provide information. 2.2 Use pictures and context to make predictions.	Edit It!, 153

Strand Ladder #5

Proficiency: Processing or Creating Written Information
✔ Students will understand that printed materials provide information.
✔ Students will use pictures and context to make predictions.

Previous skills needed:
✔ Grade-level vocabulary skill
✔ Grade-level reading skills
✔ Dictionary and thesaurus skills
✔ Verbs, modifiers, active/passive voice

Grade	Standard	Activity, game number
9/10	*Writing* 1.2 Use precise language, action verbs, sensory details, appropriate modifiers and active voice.	Voices, 134 Show Me More!, 131 Predict the End, 154 Find It Fast!, 162 Do It!, 109 Dictionary Race, 163 Difficult Duos, 124 Scavenger Hunt, 164
8	*Reading* 1.3 Use word meanings within context and show ability to verify those meanings. *Writing* 1.6 Revise for word choice.	End-Rhyme Scene, 50 The General's Ladder, 44 RatioMinute, 176 Show Me More!, 131 Speed Reader I, 115 Speed Reader II, 116

7	*Reading* 1.3 Clarify word meanings. *Writing* 1.7 Revise to improve organization and word choice.	End-Rhyme Scene, 50 The General's Ladder, 44 RatioMinute, 176 Sybil, 48
6	*Reading* 1.2 Identify and interpret figurative language. 1.5 Understand "shades of meaning." *Writing* 1.6 Revise writing for organization.	The General's Ladder, 44 Name That Sound, 19
5	*Reading* 1.2-1.5 Vocabulary development: origins, roots, figurative language. *Conventions* 1.2 Correctly use misused verbs. *Writing* 1.5 Use a thesaurus. 1.6 Revise, rearranging words and sentences.	End-Rhyme Scene, 50 The General's Ladder, 44 Name That Sound, 19 New Words, 25 Voracious Vocabulary, 51 Vocabulary Relay, 52
4	*Reading* 1.5 Use a thesaurus. 1.6 Distinguish and interpret words with multiple meanings. *Writing* 1.7 Use reference material. 1.10 Revise and edit.	Family Reunion, 21 The General's Ladder, 44 Name That Sound, 19 New Words, 25 Voracious Vocabulary, 51 Vocabulary Relay, 52

3	*Reading* 1.4-1.8 Vocabulary development. *Writing* 1.4 Revise drafts to improve coherence and logic.	Family Reunion, 21 The General's Ladder, 44 Lead Letter, 1 Name That Sound, 19 New Words, 25 Voracious Vocabulary, 51 Vocabulary Relay, 52
2	*Reading* 1.7-1.10 Vocabulary development. *Writing* 1.4 Revise drafts to improve sequence. *Conventions* 1.2 Recognize and use the correct word order in written sentences.	Family Reunion, 21 End-Rhyme Scene, 50 The General's Ladder, 44 Lead Letter, 1 Name That Sound, 19
1	*Reading* 1.3 Identify letters, words and sentences. 1.7 Classify grade-appropriate categories of words. *Writing* 1.2 Use descriptive words when writing.	Family Reunion, 21 The General's Ladder, 44 Lead Letter, 1 Name That Sound, 19
K	*Reading* 1.2 Follow words left to right, top to bottom. 1.4 Recognize that sentences are made up of separate words.	Family Reunion, 21 The General's Ladder, 44 Lead Letter, 1 Name That Sound, 19

Strand Ladder #6

Proficiency: Active and Passive Voice
✔ Students will understand the difference between active and passive voice and use active voice in writing.

Previous skills needed:
✔ Understanding of subject, object, "be" verb, past participle

Grade	Standard	Activity, game number
9/10	*Writing* 1.2 Use the active voice. *Conventions* 1.3 Demonstrate an understanding of proper English usage.	Voices, 134 To Be or Not to Be, 62
8	*Conventions* 1.1 Use correct and varied sentence types.	Junior Sentence Types, 101 Name That Sentence, 93 Edit It!, 153 What It Is!, 112 Sentence Rotations, 106 Pyramid Story, 103
7	*Conventions* 1.1 Place modifiers properly and use the active voice.	Voices, 134 Edit It!, 153
6	*Conventions* 1.2 Identify and properly use verb tenses ("to be").	Tense Exchanges, 72 Edit It!, 153
5	Add sophistication to all previous skills.	Edit It!, 153 This Part Only!, 56 Sentence Rotations, 106 Parts of Speech Relay, 75

4	*Conventions* 1.1 Use simple and compound sentences. 1.3 Identify and use regular and irregular verbs. (Identify present and past participles.)	Name That Sentence, 93 Edit It!, 153 Sentence Rotations, 106
3	*Conventions* 1.3 Identify and use verb tenses properly. 1.4 Identify and use subjects and verbs correctly.	Parts of Speech Relay, 75 This Part Only!, 56 Edit It!, 153
2	*Writing* 1.4 Revise drafts to improve sequence. *Conventions* 1.3 Identify and use various parts of speech.	Parts of Speech Relay, 75 This Part Only!, 56 Edit It!, 153
1	*Conventions* 1.1 Write and speak in complete, coherent sentences.	Edit It!, 153
K	*Writing* 1.1 Use letters and phonetically spelled words to write. *Conventions* 1.1 Recognize and use complete, coherent sentences when speaking.	Edit It!, 153

Strand Ladder #7

Proficiency: Sentence Structure
✔ Students will be able to identify and use the four sentence types.

Previous skills needed:
✔ Understand simple, compound, complex and compound/complex sentences
✔ Understand phrase and clause, predicate and subject

Grade	Standard	Activity, game number
9/10	*Conventions* 1.1 Correctly use clauses, phrases, and mechanics of punctuation. 1.3 Demonstrate understanding of proper English usage.	Scene without ..., 76 Pyramid Story, 103 Switch, 59 Dropout, 57
8	*Conventions* 1.1 Use correct and varied sentence types.	Sentence Rotations, 106 Now I'm Done, 96
7	*Conventions* 1.3 Identify all parts of speech and types and structure of sentences.	Sentence Scramble, 157 Parts Expert, 60 Parts Idiot, 61 Honk, 55 Human Sentences, 121 Parts of Speech Relay, 75
6	*Conventions* 1.1 Use simple, compound and compound-complex sentences.	Name That Sentence I and II, 93, 100

5	*Conventions* 1.1 Identify and correctly use phrases and clauses.	Counting Clauses, 69
4	*Conventions* 1.1 Use simple and compound sentences. 1.2 Combine sentences with phrases.	Junior Sentence Types, 101 Name That Sentence, 93
3	*Conventions* 1.2 Identify subjects and verbs that are in agreement.	Describe It!, 99 Half Thought/Whole Thought, 98 Parts of Speech Relay, 75 Point the Part, 53 Sentence Charade, 94
2	*Conventions* 1.1 Distinguish between complete and incomplete sentences.	Describe It!, 99 Half Thought/Whole Thought, 98 Parts of Speech Relay, 75 Point the Part, 53 Sentence Charade, 94
1	*Conventions* 1.1 Write and speak in complete sentences.	Half Thought/Whole Thought, 98
K	*Conventions* 1.1 Recognize and use complete, coherent sentences when speaking.	Half Thought/Whole Thought, 98

Strand Ladder #8

Proficiency: Proper Word Choice
✔ Students will be able to identify and correctly use the following sets of words: their, they're, there; except, accept; then, than; it's, its.

Previous skills needed:
✔ Knowledge of the targeted words
✔ Grade-level reading skill
✔ Spelling for grade level

Grade	Standard	Activity, game number
9/10	*Language Conventions* 1.3 Demonstrate understanding of proper English usage and control of grammar.	Homonee-Quips, 47 All Together Now!, 8 Contraction Action, 171 Edit It!, 153
8	*Language Conventions* 1.6 Use correct spelling conventions.	Homonee-Quips, 47 All Together Now!, 8 Contraction Action, 171 Edit It!, 153
7	Add sophistication to previously learned skills.	Homonee-Quips, 47 All Together Now!, 8 Contraction Action, 171 Edit It!, 153
6	*Language Conventions* 1.5 Spell frequently misspelled words correctly.	Homonee-Quips, 47 All Together Now!, 8 Contraction Action, 171 Edit It!, 153

5	*Reading* 1.3 Understand and explain frequently used synonyms, antonyms and homographs. *Language Conventions* 1.5 Spell contractions correctly.	All Together Now!, 8 Contraction Action, 171 Edit It!, 153 Homonee-Quips, 47
4	Add sophistication to previously learned skills.	All Together Now!, 8 Contraction Action, 171 Edit It!, 153 Homonee-Quips, 47
3	*Reading* 1.4 Use knowledge of antonyms, synonyms, homophones, homographs. *Language Conventions* 1.8 Spell correctly.	All Together Now!, 8 Contraction Action, 171 Edit It!, 153
2	*Language Conventions* 1.7 Spell frequently used, irregular words.	All Together Now!, 8 Contraction Action, 171 Edit It!, 153
1	*Language Conventions* 1.3 Identify and correctly use contractions. 1.8 Spell appropriately for grade level.	All Together Now!, 8 Contraction Action, 171 Edit It!, 153
K	*Language Conventions* 1.1 Recognize and use complete, coherent sentences when speaking.	All Together Now!, 8 Contraction Action, 171 Edit It!, 153

Strand Ladder #9

Proficiency: Subject/Verb Agreement
✔ Students will demonstrate knowledge and understanding of subject/verb agreement in speaking and writing.

Previous skills needed:
✔ Eight parts of speech
✔ Subject/noun
✔ Predicate
✔ Complete sentences

Grade	Standard	Activity, game number
9/10	1.2 Understand sentence construction and proper usage (i.e., consistency of verb tenses). 1.3 Demonstrate an understanding of proper English usage and control of grammar.	Alpha-Parts, 73 Don't Get Tense, 71 Dropout I and II, 57, 58 Edit It!, 153 Half Thought/Whole Thought, 98 Parts of Speech Relay, 75
8	1.4 Edit written manuscripts to ensure that correct grammar is used.	Don't Get Tense, 71 Dropout I and II, 57, 58 Edit It!, 153 Half Thought/Whole Thought, 98 Parts of Speech Relay, 75
7	1.3 Identify all parts of speech. 1.4 Demonstrate appropriate English usage.	Alpha-Parts, 73 Don't Get Tense, 71 Dropout I and II, 57, 58 Edit It!, 153 Half Thought/Whole Thought, 98 Parts of Speech Relay, 75

6	1.2 Identify and properly use verb tenses; ensure that verb tenses agree with compound subjects.	Describe It!, 99 Edit It!, 153 Half Thought/Whole Thought, 98 Parts of Speech Relay, 75
5	Add sophistication to previous knowledge and skills.	Describe It!, 99 Edit It!, 153 Half Thought/Whole Thought, 98 Parts of Speech Relay, 75
4	1.3 Identify and use regular and irregular verbs in writing and speaking.	Describe It!, 99 Edit It!, 153 Half Thought/Whole Thought, 98 Parts of Speech Relay, 75
3	1.2 Identify subjects and verbs that are in agreement. 1.4 Identify and use subjects and verbs correctly.	Describe It!, 99 Edit It!, 153 Half Thought/Whole Thought, 98 Parts of Speech Relay, 75
2	1.1 Distinguish between complete and incomplete sentences. 1.2 Use correct word order in sentences. 1.3 Identify and correctly use various parts of speech.	Describe It!, 99 Edit It!, 153 Half Thought/Whole Thought, 98 Parts of Speech Relay, 75
1	1.1 Write and speak in complete sentences. 1.2 Identify and correctly use singular and plural nouns.	Describe It!, 99 Edit It!, 153 Half Thought/Whole Thought, 98

| K | 1.0 Students write and speak with a command of standard English convention.
1.1 Recognize and use complete, coherent sentences when speaking. | Describe It!, 99
Edit It!, 153
Half Thought/Whole Thought, 98
Parts of Speech Relay, 75 |

Strand Ladder #10

Proficiency: Writing a Cohesive Paper
✔ Students will be able to create a thesis and maintain unity in a piece of original writing.

Previous skills needed:
✔ Thesis
✔ Main Idea
✔ Paragraphing
✔ Structure

Grade	Standard	Activity, game number
9/10	*Writing* 1.1 Establish a controlling impression/thesis. 1.9 Revise writing to improve logic and coherence.	Thesis Thought, 158 Transition Position, 156 Speech Spasm, 135 Speak!, 144 Edit It!, 153 Jigsaw, 102 Stand and Deliver, 68
8	*Writing* 1.1 Have a coherent thesis and clear, well-supported conclusion. 1.2 Establish coherence among paragraphs through transitions, parallel structure and writing techniques.	Thesis Thought, 158 Transition Position, 156 Human Sentences, 121 Jigsaw, 102 Stand and Deliver, 68 Edit It!, 153 Speak!, 144

7	*Writing* 1.1 Create an organizational structure and use effective transitions. 1.3 Use note-taking, outlining and summarizing to impose structure.	Transition Position, 156 Human Sentences, 121 Jigsaw, 102 Edit It!, 153 Speak!, 144
6	*Writing* 1.2 Create multiple-paragraph expository compositions. 1.3 Use a variety of effective and coherent organizational patterns.	Human Sentences, 121 Jigsaw, 102 Edit It!, 153
5	*Writing* 1.1 Create multiple-paragraph narrative compositions. 1.2 Create multiple-paragraph expository compositions.	Human Sentences, 121 Jigsaw, 102 Edit It!, 153 What's the Form?, 108
4	*Writing* 1.1 Select focus and organizational pattern. 1.2 Create multiple-paragraph compositions. 1.3 Use traditional structure.	Human Sentences, 121

3	*Writing* 1.1 Create a single paragraph. 1.4 Revise drafts to improve coherence and logic.	Human Sentences, 121
2	*Writing* 1.1 Group related ideas and maintain a consistent focus. *Conventions* 1.1 Distinguish between complete and incomplete sentences.	Half Thought/Whole Thought, 98 Name That Sentence, 93 What It Is!, 112 Word Sort, 36
1	*Writing* 1.1 Select a focus when writing. *Conventions* 1.1 Write and speak in coherent, complete sentences	Half Thought/Whole Thought, 98 Name That Sentence, 93 What It Is!, 112 Word Sort, 36
K	*Writing* 1.3 Write by moving from left to right and from top to bottom.	Human Sentences (simplified), 121

Testing for Learning

During the 2000-2001 school year I was involved in a research project with a number of teachers in the northern region of California. My work with Maryel Roberts at Meadow View School in Susanville, CA, helped me see a relationship between multiple-choice testing and written demonstrations of language skills that I'd never seen so clearly before.

She set up a pre- and post-test for her Grammar Wars lesson teaching punctuation and capitals in sentences with quotations. Her test had multiple-choice questions and two items that required students to create their own sentences with punctuation, capitals and quotation marks. To make a short story even shorter, students demonstrated "learning" the content in multiple-choice questions before they could demonstrate those same skills in their own writing. Did I word that clearly? If learning takes time (and it certainly does), the first arena for success with a lot of knowledge and skills is multiple-choice. It's an easier demonstration, I think, for several reasons. One, so much information is given in each question itself, and in the questions that come before and after. Two, many of the questions are very simple. Three, good diagnostic, multiple-choice questions try to focus on only one particular skill or fact. Students rarely have to create anything simple or complex, because everything is already written. Writing, however, requires the student to do it all, and nothing exists on the blank paper prior to the student beginning. Point?

When you do Grammar Wars well, you will be actively engaged during the lesson's activities in looking for the learning demonstrations that are to be repeated and/or reinforced in that activity. Are they processing the new terms? Are they repeating them over and over so that they'll remember them? Are they hearing subject/verb combinations over and over so they will be able (with the next few activities and instruction) to count clauses in sentences with their ears?

Now I know enough from the multiple-choice and written test information to know that verbal demonstration of knowledge and skills may not transfer to multiple-choice or written demonstrations.

Learning takes time and it travels differently for different students. So I want to use multiple-choice somewhere in my lesson, probably earlier than later to assess *their skills and knowledge on paper.* And I'm going to assess my students/actors in the performance activities to see how they are doing kinesthetically (knowing there may or may not be a correlation).

Now if your district is really into norm testing, then multiple-choice might be all you have to do. However, if student writing (and reading) is the long-term proficiency that your district and the world expect of your students, then you need to build your lessons and design the ending tests to reflect the demonstrations for which your curriculum strives.

Activities can look like learning, and Grammar Wars can trick a lot of people, but the best application for English/language arts teachers takes the kids through a process with a lot of good assessments leading to a proficiency that is what good education provides. Activities are fine; learning is the goal. Multiple-choice testing shows a stage in learning. Applied, multi-task demonstrations are more complete demonstrations of learning.

Appendices

The appendices include samples and forms which
may be copied or reproduced.

Sample Weave Model

Pre-test on Misplaced Modifiers

Direct instruction of fact/skill/concept

Misplaced Modifier
- ✔ Defined
- ✔ Correct and incorrect sentence
- ✔ SAT9 second example
- ✔ Two sentences: one correct and one
  with misplaced modifier

Page   **Stage**

Activity #1 — Understanding assessed —
non-game

- ✔ Write a descriptive sentence at your
  desk; now write a version with a
  misplaced modifier. Circle the
  misplaced modifier.

Activity #2 — Knowledge/skill description

- ✔ Define *misplaced modifier.*
- ✔ Teacher samples used for a team
  competition. Sample sentences
  projected onto the board. Group must
  come to consensus, or first small
  group to decide honks and declares.

Page	**Stage**

Activity #3 — Written demonstration with teams, timed

- ✔ SAT9 multiple-choice form done in pairs (teacher-matched pairs). Pairs timed, with penalties for missed items.
- ✔ Answers reviewed in class and scores tabulated.

Activity #4 — Performance application

- ✔ Students, in pairs in front, make up a sentence, first with correct modification, and second with a modifier misplaced.
- ✔ Competition where pairs are given thirty seconds to give a sentence and its revision with misplaced modifiers.

Activity #5 — Written work for competition

- ✔ Pairs write ten sentences with misplaced modifiers.
- ✔ Misplaced modifiers are checked by teacher or other pair (a pair not using the list in the next activity).

Activity #6 — Competition using student prepared materials

- ✔ **College Bowl:** Teams (pairs) compete against other pairs. One team reads its list of ten and the guessing team must identify the misplaced modifiers correctly in sixty seconds. (Sentences can be read or projected on a screen.)

Page	**Stage**

Activity #7 — Written demonstration

✔ SAT9 multiple-choice form done alone.
✔ Answers reviewed.

**Activity #8 — Written or performed to
respond to #7 assessment**

✔ If #7 permits verbal applications —
two-person scenes where the actors
try to use as many sentences with
misplaced modifiers as possible. One
point per misplaced modifier.
Audience members honk at each one
to earn additional audience points.

Activity #9 — Proven Skill Competence

✔ SAT9 multiple-choice form done alone
for credit.

Sample Vocabulary Bingo Card

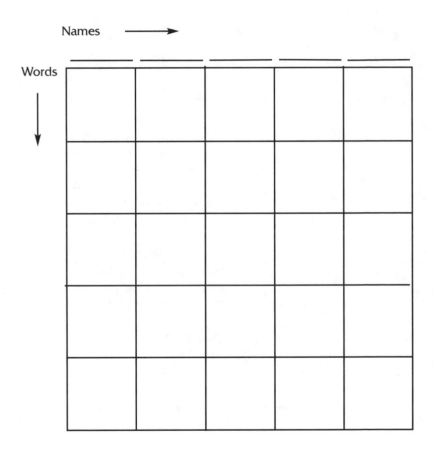

Names ⟶

Words ↓

Scavenger Hunt II Sample

Count the number of adverbs, conjunctions and prepositions in the paragraph below. Write the numbers you've counted on the corresponding lines at the bottom of the page.

The thoughtful man constantly lives in his fantasies because life is too rough, and he cannot deal with it except in isolation. He lingers in his memory of the beautiful daffodils. They are his one true pleasure in life. The flowers are magical and represent hope. The narrator's solitary existence allows him to take extra time and admire the small things in life.

_____	_____	_____
adverbs	**conjunctions**	**prepositions**

Sample Assembly Script (four teams)

Remember: Only a small percentage of audience members have improv experience.

Materials:
- ✔ Three robes
- ✔ Three sets of scoring numbers
- ✔ Scoreboard
- ✔ Team name cards (pre-filled out)
- ✔ Clipboard with agenda (pen)
- ✔ Stopwatch
- ✔ Horn

Placement:
Four four-person teams in the wings (teams 1 and 2 in right wing; 3 and 4 in left wing). Judges in the wings in robes.

1. Emcee introduction (some actor behind the curtains)
2. Welcome
3. Introduce teams 1 and 2
   a. They bring in the name cards to be hung on the scoreboard
4. Team captains lead team introductions with style
   a. Teams sit in one-quarter positions in Upstage Right and Left positions
5. Introduction of judges and explanation of scoring categories
6. National anthem ("Flintstone's" theme)

Game:	**Judges' criteria:**

1. Professor Know-It-All (period honk)
   a. Two teams
2. Mutants (narrative structure)
   a. Two teams
3. Alphabet Scene (alphabet, vocabulary *option*)
   a. Warm-ups
      i. Two actors time letter at a time
      ii. Two audience members time letter at a time
      iii. Two audience members are letter judges (honk if out of sequence)
   b. Alphabet scene — ninety seconds
      i. Two teams
4. Murder (adjectives, prepositional phrases)
   a. Two teams (two- or three-member teams based on time left)
5. Scene without a Letter (rotation, elimination) (vocabulary/synonyms, euphemisms)
6. Winners announced
7. Winning team gets to do a thank you duet poem!

Judges' criteria:
Entertain, Technique, Periods
Entertain, Technique, Narrative
Entertain, Technique, Narrative
Entertain, Technique
Elimination

Grammar Wars Assembly Script

Materials:
- ✔ Four sets of judges' scorecards
- ✔ Lists for timed lists (coordinating conjunctions, subordinating conjunctions, etc.)
- ✔ Cards for ten-word complex or compound sentences
- ✔ Names of audience members with English/language arts backgrounds
- ✔ Microphone off-stage to start the show
- ✔ Cards with things to *omit* in "Scene without a ..."
- ✔ Chart stand with pens
  Pre-written items:
  - Sentence Rotations
  - Spell-Well Graphic for demonstration
  - Syntax Rotations
- ✔ Stopwatch
- ✔ Horn bar and horns

Before show:
- ✔ Judges get ten-word complex or compound sentences from audience members.
- ✔ Ask for names of audience members who know punctuation of syntax types, quotations marks, names of regular verbs.

Act One

Introductions: (Two teams, judges and emcee are off-stage)
1. Emcee introduced by actor off-stage on microphone.
2. Team captains introduced by off-stage actor.
3. Captains introduce their teams (use audience introduction style).
4. Judges introduced by off-stage actor.
5. Scoring explained (entertainment, technical, narrative, language skills) by off-stage actor.

Round #1 — Teams #1 and #2

Emcee Games Parts of Speech, Clauses, Spelling	**Notes**
✔ Timed Lists Coordinating conjunctions Subordinating conjunctions	Possibly the judges' list from the audience before the show
✔ Tag Team (Parts of Speech), team members only	Each team competes once.
✔ Tag Team II (Parts of Speech) with audience member	Each team competes once with an *audience member who looks smart.* Timed Judges score complete list and correct examples.
✔ Scene without a … Pronoun Preposition Form of "to be" Etc.	Two players, each from an opposing team
✔ One Voice	Compounds in forty-five seconds (with punctuation, with horns) Each team sends up two actors.
✔ Rotation scene (sentence type)	Rotation order on chart-stand paper Judges honk.
✔ Pyramid Story (1-2-3-2-1) As many complete pyramids as possible	Four actors come up and one member directs for number of clauses. Ninety-second time limits Judges honk for errors. Judges count complete pyramids.

✔ Spell-Well	Explain with written examples on the chart-stand paper. Judges write words. Judges honk on errors.
✔ Spell-Well with audience member	

Winner announced.

Round #2 — Teams #3 and #4

Introductions of Teams #3 and #4
1. Captains first
2. Captains introduce team members (like a football team set of intros and a rap intro)

Emcee Games Alphabet, Punctuation, Syntax	**Notes**
✔ Alphabet — timed lists One at a time Two at a time Without vowels	Five-second penalty for incorrect letters, placements or omissions
✔ Alphabet with audience member	Both pairs of competing teams are standing in front at the same time.
✔ Scene without a Letter (rotation) All team members compete.	The team with the highest number of "honked" actors in two minutes earns low score. Judge scores for technique. Actors can be honked for stalling.
✔ Alphabet Scene (ninety seconds)	Each team does with its own pair.

✔ Syntax Twins (simple, compound, complex)	Two teams compete separately.
✔ Punctuation Spasm	Scores for correct punctuations.
✔ Cooking with Mutants (with assigned sentence types)	I.e., One team is assigned compound, and the other complex or simple sentences.
✔ Professor Know-it-All with punctuation	Scored on capitals and periods and any internal needs. Each actor (four) has a horn. All answers must have four sentences and the perfect answer has each of the four sentences end with a different actor so each has honked their horn.
✔ Edith Edit	Audience member is used as Edith with the horns. Or, each team picks someone in the audience to honk on punctuation rules. Two actors converse (with Edith between them) and Edith (or they) have to punctuate the conversation correctly. Or, two audience members converse (actor Edith between them) and the actor has to punctuate correctly — sixty seconds.

Winner is announced.

Intermission

Act Two

Round #3 — Winners

Emcee Games Narrative, Grammar	Notes
✔ Story, Story, Out (styles)	Styles from audience
✔ Typewriter	Conflict from the audience
✔ Movie Pitch	Movie type from audience
✔ Dropout (subject-verb agreement)	
✔ To Be or Not to Be	
✔ Slide Show	Ask audience for an event from their lives with a problem.
✔ Family Reunion	Family reunion gone bad Bad date Vacation gone bad
✔ A Day in the Life	Character from audience
✔ Point of View	Harold
✔ Cooking with Mutants	
✔ Tone Zones (Stage areas are assigned an emotional quality.)	The list comes from the audience.
✔ Best bedtime story with a new moral	(As told to a little child — typewriter-ish)

Introduce winning teams.

Round #3 *(No repeats from Round #1)*	Game	Notes
✔ Emcee Choice #1		
✔ Emcee Choice #2		
✔ Team #1 Challenge		
✔ Emcee Choice #3		
✔ Team #2 Challenge		

Winning team celebrates.

Team Documents

Preparing Team Players for Specializing

Prior to conducting the competition, ask the teams to plan which actors will be specialists for which games so that when games are announced during the show, there is no time or performance momentum lost in team members jumping to the stage to begin.

Captain: _____

Members: _____

_____

_____

_____

Round #1 — Teams #1 and #2

Emcee Games Parts of Speech, Clauses, Spelling	Actors	Rules	Specialists
✔ Timed Lists Coordinating conjunctions Subordinating conjunctions		Possibly the judge's list from the audience before the show	1 or 2 actors
✔ Tag Team (Parts of Speech), team members only		Each team competes once.	2 actors
✔ Tag Team II (Parts of Speech) with audience member		Each team competes once with an *audience member who looks smart.* Timed Judges score complete list and correct examples.	2 actors

Emcee Games	Actors	Rules	Specialists
✔ Scene without … Pronoun Preposition Form of "to be" Etc.		Two players, each from an opposing team	2 actors
✔ One Voice		Compounds in 45 seconds (with punctuation, with *horns*) Each team competes with two actors.	2 actors
✔ Rotation Scene (sentence type)		Rotation order on chart-stand paper Judges honk.	All players
✔ Pyramid Story (1-2-3-4-3-2-1) As many complete pyramids as possible		4 actors up and 1 member directs for number of clauses. 90-second time limit Judges honk for errors. Judges count complete pyramids.	Director 4 actors
✔ Spell-Well		Explain with written examples on the chart-stand paper. Judges write words. Judges honk on errors.	2 actors
✔ Spell-Well with audience member			1 actor

Winner announced.

Round #2 — Teams #3 and #4

Emcee Games Alphabet, Punctuation, Syntax	Actors	Rules	Specialists
✔ Alphabet — timed lists One at a time Two at a time Without vowels		Five-second penalty for incorrect letters, placements or omissions	2 actors
✔ Alphabet with audience member		Both pairs of competing teams are standing in front at the same time.	1 actor
✔ Scene without a Letter (rotation) All team members compete.		The team with the highest number of "honked" actors in two minutes earns low score. Judge scores for technique. Actors can be honked for stalling.	All players
✔ Alphabet Scene (90 seconds)		Each team does with its own pair.	2 actors
✔ Syntax Twins (simple, compound, complex)		Two teams compete separately.	2 actors
✔ Punctuation Spasm		Scores for correct punctuations.	2 actors

Emcee Games	Actors	Rules	Specialists
✔ Cooking with Mutants (with assigned sentence types)		I.e., one team is assigned compounds, and the other complexes or simples.	2 actors
✔ Professor Know-It-All with punctuation		Scored on capitals and periods and any internal needs. Each actor (four) has a horn. All answers must have four sentences and the perfect answer has each of the four sentences end with a different actor so each has honked their horn.	All actors
✔ Edith Edit		Audience member is used as Edith with the horns. Or, each team picks someone in the audience to honk on punctuation rules. Two actors converse (with Edith between them) and Edith (or they) have to punctuate the conversation correctly. Or, two audience members converse (actor Edith between them) and the actor has to punctuate correctly — 60 seconds.	2 actors *or* 1 actor

Round #3 — Winners

Emcee Games Narrative, Grammar	Actors	Rules	Specialists
✔ Story, Story, Out (styles)		Styles from audience	Director 4 actors
✔ Typewriter		Conflict is from the audience.	Writer Actors
✔ Movie Pitch		Movie type from audience	Critics Actors
✔ Dropout (subject-verb agreement)			2 actors
✔ To Be or Not to Be			2 actors
✔ Slide Show		Ask audience for an event from their lives with a problem.	Narrator Actors

Emcee Games	Actors	Rules	Specialists
✔ Family Reunion		Family reunion gone bad Bad date Vacation gone bad	2 actors
✔ A Day in the Life		Character from audience	Narrator Actors
✔ Point of View		Harold	3 actors
✔ Cooking with Mutants			2 actors
✔ Tone Zones (Stage areas are assigned an emotional quality.)		The list comes from the audience.	3 actors
✔ Best bedtime story with a new moral		(As told to a little child — typewriter-ish)	Narrator Actors

Micetro Assembly Script

Materials:

- ✔ Scoreboard
- ✔ Actors' names in laminate
- ✔ Cards with actors' names
- ✔ Chart stand
- ✔ Microphone
- ✔ Two stools
- ✔ Horn bar

Act One

Introductions: (Twelve players, scorekeeper, judge(s), director and emcee are off-stage)

1. Emcee introduced by actor off-stage on microphone.
2. Players are introduced.
3. Judge(s) introduced.
4. Director introduced.
5. Scorekeeper introduced.
6. Scoring explained (audience applauds — 1, 2, 3 for entertainment; judge(s) vote — 1, 2, 3 for technical, narrative).
7. Players put their names in a hat.
8. Emcee has an audience member pull two (or three) names for the first scene.

Games	Judge's Criteria	Notes
✔ Advancing Ladder	Mime Advancing	Upper stage Director
✔ Duet Poems	Rhythm Rhyme	Upper stage Microphone
✔ Scene without a Letter	C.R.O.W.E. Avoiding letter Good pace	Judge (honks)
✔ Murder (must mime murdering an inanimate object in an unusual way.)	Mime Energy Facing audience Creativity	Upper stage
✔ Emotional Body Parts	Body expression Consistent emotional work C.R.O.W.E.	Upper stage Director
✔ Too Intense for Words	C.R.O.W.E. Subtext	Lower stage Director
✔ Voice Over (physical actors are judged.)	Accepting Enhancing offers	Upper stage Microphone Director
✔ Movie Pitch (physical actors are judged.)	Accepting Enhancing offers	Upper stage Director
✔ Scene without Laughter	C.R.O.W.E. Avoiding humor No clever ideas Tone control	Lower stage Director

Games	Judge's Criteria	Notes
✔ Reverse (lines are said in reverse.)	Reversed lines are opposite Consistent C.R.O.W.E.	Upper stage
✔ A Day in the Life	C.R.O.W.E. Using all the offers from audience Form	Upper stage Director
✔ Scene Based on a Moral Dilemma	C.R.O.W.E. Crisis	Upper stage Director
✔ First Line, Last Line	C.R.O.W.E. Doing first and last line	Upper stage
✔ Point of View	C.R.O.W.E. Accepting	Upper stage Spotlights (3)
✔ Point of View (each does two parts — could be two characters.)	C.R.O.W.E.	Upper stage Spotlights
✔ Forward/Reverse (must say lines in reverse order when director says "reverse" and in forward order when director says "forward.")	Line sequences play correctly forward and in reverse	Upper stage

Games	Judge's Criteria	Notes
✔ Secrets (three actors with initial interior monologs that reveal secrets that are used in a scene)	C.R.O.W.E.	Upper stage Spotlights Director
✔ Animal Scene	C.R.O.W.E. Playing the animal characteristics for your human character	Upper stage Director
✔ Scene with Bad Mime/Good Mime (shifts are made with director's command, "Good mime!" or "Bad mime!")	C.R.O.W.E. Mime (as required)	Upper stage Director
✔ Family Reunion	C.R.O.W.E. Mime Speed	Upper stage Director

Round #1 is over when all actors have played. Scores are reviewed, and the top six or eight actors are identified. Round #2 is played with the same list of games with unplayed titles (no repeats). After each actor has performed and been scored one time (or two times if fast), scores are reviewed, and the top three or four actors are identified for the final round.

Intermission/Act Two

Round #3 continues with the unplayed games from Act One until all actors have performed two times.

Final scenes might be surprise solo scenes:
1. Love scene with an object
2. Final scene from a tragic sci-fi-opera
3. Death scene close-up from a low-budget film
4. Finger puppet scene from a Broadway musical

Scores are given. Totals are tallied and the winner is chosen.

Team Competition Performance (two teams)

Materials:

- ✔ Two stools (right proscenium)
- ✔ Rehearsal furniture (general in wings)
- ✔ Microphone (right proscenium)
- ✔ Horn bar
- ✔ Horns
- ✔ Stopwatch
- ✔ Chart stand
- ✔ Props
- ✔ "What's in a Minute" lists
  (prepared before performance with audience)
- ✔ Judges' robes
- ✔ Judges' score cards
- ✔ Scoreboard
- ✔ Team names (for scoreboard)
- ✔ Give-away T-shirts

Act One

Introductions: (Two teams, judges and emcee are off-stage)

1. Emcee introduced by actor off-stage on microphone.
2. Team captains are introduced.
3. Captains introduce their teams (use audience introduction style).
4. Judges introduced.
5. Scoring explained (entertainment, technical, narrative).

Emcee Games Entertainment, Technical, Narrative	Actors	Rules	Notes
✔ Story, Story, Out (styles: audience opinion)	4 + 1	Four up and one sitter Each of four has a style. Audience chooses death or slow motion torture.	
✔ Movie Pitch	All	Two reviewers Two actors	
✔ Scene without a Letter	All	Both teams play (1-4). Violations are counted. Technique is judged.	
✔ Sound Effects	2	Two-person team Microphone	
✔ Scene without Laughter	All	Lower stage Two-person scene Teams on the sides Rotations Technique judged	
✔ Slide Show	1 + 3	Narrator at microphone Three on-stage in dark Light operator works cues.	
✔ Point of View	3	Three spiked spots Harold the start Sixty-second monologs	
✔ Reverse (statement)	2	Two-person scenes Emcee calls	

Emcee Games	Actors	Rules	Notes
✔ Typewriter	1 + 3	Audience gives the conflict type.	
✔ Day in the Life	1 + 3	Narrator Audience content is gathered. Audience member is asked if they want a different ending to the "day."	
✔ Family Reunion	2 (or 3)	Horn bar Family reunion, great or bad date, romantic vacation	
✔ Murder (see Belt & Stockley, "Chain Murder Endowments," p. 168)	2	L.O.W.	

Winner announced.

Round #2

Introductions of Teams #3 and #4
1. Captains first
2. Captains introduce team members (like football team intros and a rap intro).

Round #2 (No repeats from #1)	Game	
✔ Emcee Choice #1		
✔ Emcee Choice #2		
✔ Team #1 Challenge		
✔ Emcee Choice #3		
✔ Team #2 Challenge		

Winner announced.

Intermission

Act Two

Emcee Games	Team Challenge Games
✔ Cooking with Mutants	
✔ Alphabet Pairs (words)	
✔ N-Word Sentences	
✔ Best Scene Based on a Moral Dilemma (audience idea)	
✔ Punctuate Yourself	

Team Documents

Preparing Team Players for Specializing

Prior to conducting the competition, ask the teams to plan which actors will be specialists for which games so that when games are announced during the show, there is no time or performance momentum lost in team members jumping to the stage to begin.

Captain: _____

Members: _____

_____

_____

_____

Emcee Games Entertainment, Technical, Narrative	Actors	Rules	Specialists
✔ Story, Story, Out ✔ Styles: Audience opinion		Four up and one pointer Each of four has a style. Audience chooses death or slow motion torture.	All players
✔ Movie Pitch		Two reviewers two actors	Speakers Actors
✔ Scene without a Letter		Both teams play (1-4). Violations are counted. Technique is judged.	All players
✔ Sound Effects		Two-person team Microphone	Sound Actor

Emcee Games	Actors	Rules	Specialists
✔ Scene without Laughter		Lower stage Two-person scene Teams on the sides Rotations Technique judged	All players
✔ Slide Show		Narrator at microphone Three on-stage in dark Light operator works cues.	Narrator Actors
✔ Point of View		Three spiked spots Harold the start 60-second monologs.	3 actors
✔ Reverse (statement)		Two-person scenes. Emcee calls.	2 actors
✔ Typewriter		Audience gives the conflict type.	Writer Actors
✔ Day in the Life		Typewriter Audience content is gathered. Audience member is asked if they want a different ending to the "day."	Writer Actors
✔ Family Reunion		Horn bar Family reunion, great or bad date, romantic vacation	2-3 actors
✔ Murder		Low	2 actors

Team Challenge Games			
Game	**Actors**	**Rules**	**Specialists**
✔ Advancing Ladder		Competitive Audience idea	1 actor
✔ Props		Two pairs alternate ideas.	2 actors
✔ Duet Poems		Confident Character choices Rhythm Rhyme Audience idea	2 actors
✔ What's in a Minute (generated in the audience prior to the game)		Charades Mime Gibberish Sound Effects Hummed melodies	Mime Team
✔ Scene without Laughter		Rotation Count errors for score Technical score by judge	All players
✔ Alphabet Scene		Two from same team 90 seconds	2 actors
✔ Alphabet Words list (audience category, "I bet we can do it in less than … ")		Two from same team 90 seconds (or less)	2 actors
✔ Either of the Alphabet items with an audience member		Two from same team 90 seconds	1 actor

Act Two Emcee Games			
Game	**Actors**	**Rules**	**Specialists**
✔ Cooking with Mutants		Four sentences The Form	2 actors
✔ Alphabet Pairs (words)		Two players with audience ideas Fastest time	2 actors
✔ N-Word Sentences		Two players 90 seconds	2 actors
✔ Best Scene Based on a Moral Dilemma (audience idea)		2-minute maximum	Team
✔ Punctuate Yourself		90-second (or less) scene	2 actors

Competition Bracket Samples

Two-team Competition

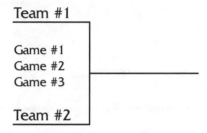

Team #1

Game #1
Game #2
Game #3

Team #2

Three-team Competition

Team #1

Game #1
Game #2
Game #3

Team #2

Team #3

Bye

Winner #1

Game #4
Game #5
Game #6

Team #3

Winner #2

Four-team Competition

Team #1

Game #1
Game #2   Winner #1
Game #3

Team #2

                    Game #7   Winner
                    Game #8
Team #3   Game #9

Game #4
Game #5   Winner #2
Game #6

Team #4

Five-team Competition

Team #1

Game #1
Game #2
Game #3

Team #2

Winner #1

Team #3

Game #4
Game #5
Game #6

Team #4

Winner #2

Game #7
Game #8
Game #9

Winner #3

Team #5

Bye

Team #5

Winner

Six-team Competition

Six-team Double Elimination Tournament

Ready-to-win Brackets

Winners' Brackets

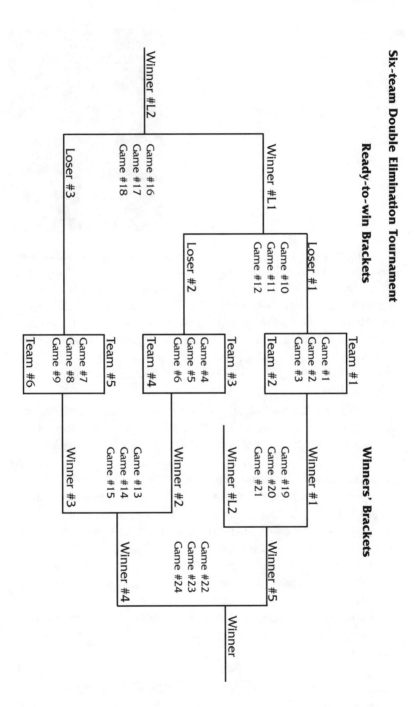

About the Author

Tom Ready has been teaching theatre and language arts for the past twenty years at Lassen High School, Lassen Community College, Chico State, and within the Arts-in-Corrections program at CCC Susanville, and High Desert State Prison. He has worked as a theatre consultant for the California Arts Project, the Northeast California Arts Project, and various counties in northern California. He presents workshops, consults, and is a conference speaker with educational and state organizations in the areas of team building, restructuring, and systems thinking.

He enjoys producing original theatrical works, in recent years working with Snail Records in Chicago on a production of Ken Nordine's *Word Jazz*, and Ruth Gendler's *The Book of Qualities*.

In 1990 he appeared in a Malpaso production of Clint Eastwood's *Pink Cadillac* with Bernadette Peters.

He recently finished a collaborative theatre project with Dr. William Torch, pediatric neurologist at Washoe Medical Center in Reno, Nevada, on an original script about child abuse and children's rights presented at Lassen High School.

Tom was awarded a national Christa McAuliffe Fellowship for the 1997-98 school year in the areas of drama, literacy, and educational restructuring.

Currently, Tom teaches acting and English, and is in charge of organizational development at Lassen High School in Susanville, California.

Order Form

Meriwether Publishing Ltd.
PO Box 7710
Colorado Springs, CO 80933-7710
Phone: (719) 594-4422 Fax: 719-5949916
Website: www.meriwether.com

Please send me the following books:

_____	**Grammar Wars II #BK-B252**	**$15.95**
	by Tom Ready	
	How to integrate improvisation and language arts	
_____	**Grammar Wars #BK-B241**	**$16.95**
	by Tom Ready	
	179 games and improvs for learning language arts	
_____	**Improve with Improv! #BK-B160**	**$14.95**
	by Brie Jones	
	A guide to improvisation and character development	
_____	**Theatre Games for Young Performers #BK-B188**	**$16.95**
	by Maria C. Novelly	
	Improvisations and exercises for developing acting skills	
_____	**Theatre Games and Beyond #BK-B217**	**$16.95**
	by Amiel Schotz	
	A creative approach for performers	
_____	**Spontaneous Performance #BK-B239**	**$15.95**
	by Marsh Cassady	
	Acting through improv	
_____	**Acting Games — Improvisations and Exercises #BK-B168**	**$16.95**
	by Marsh Cassady	
	A textbook of theatre games and improvisations	

These and other fine Meriwether Publishing books are available at your local bookstore or direct from the publisher. Prices subject to change without notice. Check our website or call for current prices.

Name: _____

Organization name: _____

Address: _____

City: _____ State: _____

Zip: _____ Phone: _____

❑ **Check enclosed**

❑ **Visa / MasterCard / Discover #** _____

Signature: _____ Expiration date: _____

(required for Visa/MasterCard/Discover orders)

Colorado residents: Please add 3% sales tax.
Shipping: Include $3.75 for the first book and 75¢ for each additional book ordered.

❑ *Please send me a copy of your complete catalog of books and plays.*